Grace Ragland   Steve Justice

DIVIDE BY ONE

A Memoir

Dedicated to:
Barry, Rosemary, and Andy Jones
All those with Multiple Sclerosis who can't,
and to those who think they can't
John Dunbar and Mike Pace

Grace Ragland would like to thank: Patti Folgman, Jill Garvin, Kym Fasczewski, Starr Affolter, Joe Caruso, Randy and Kris Whorton, Wills Ragland, Fisher Hutchens, John Rodriguez, Dan Hensley, Scott Thigpen, Scott McConnell, Dawson Wheeler, Brent Goldstein, Dan Lysk, Laurel McHargue, Tommy Reagh, Jimmy Harris, Greg Foster, Teva Neuroscience, Cahaba Cycles, Trailhead, Inc., Moab Bike Shop, Southern Carnage Bike Shop, Randolph Raiders NICA team, friends in MS, friends in biking. Extra thanks to everyone who helped me during my cancer treatments, especially Lisa Beddingfield. Lastly, a huge thanks to Steve Justice for sparking my interest with his amazing writing skills many years ago and agreeing to take on the task of helping me share my crazy story.

Steve Justice would like to thank: Vicki Justice for encouraging me to keep writing, Margaret Howell for her editing magic and wise counsel, Chris and Camille Berge/Berge Design for the great cover and layout, Laurel McHargue for sharing her title suggestion, Dawson Wheeler, Scott Thigpen, Brent Goldstein, Michael McCoy and Adventure Cycling Association, Sandy Campbell, Ben Justice, Elizabeth Howell, and finally Grace Ragland for trusting me to tell her amazing story.

PROLOGUE

The Rocky Mountains were formed some 70 million years ago in heat and violence. They are the product of two continental plates colliding and scraping across one another, thrusting rock higher and higher. The result of this massive friction is one of the most iconic and deserted landscapes in North America; the forbidding peaks forming a barrier between east and west. The bony spine of this mountain range stretches from Canada to New Mexico and divides the waters of the United States, shunting them to the Pacific on the western side or the Atlantic on the eastern side. This is called the Continental Divide.

A hiking trail was built along the divide, called descriptively yet uncreatively, the Continental Divide Trail, or CDT. The CDT is a world-renowned hiking trail and, along with the Appalachian Trail and the Pacific Crest Trail, forms one leg of what is called the Triple Crown of American long-distance hikes.

In the 1990s, the Adventure Cycling Association mapped a route for cyclists alongside the CDT. It was a patchwork of forest roads, paved county and state roads, and singletrack trail that allowed a rider to travel from the Canadian border to the Mexican border, shadowing and crossing the Divide some 32 times.

It was designed to be a scenic route for the bikepacker to savor at his or her leisure over weeks or even months. Of course, there are always those human beings among us who, with endless stamina, push the boundaries of the possible. Some of these visionaries saw the possibility of turning this pleasurable route into a masochistic race course for the adventurous, ambitious, and restless.

In 2007, that race course was extended 250 miles to Banff, Canada, and the race known as the Tour Divide was born. The profile of the race is so immense, it is hard to translate into relatable terms. The race stretches more than 2,700 miles from Banff to Antelope Wells, New Mexico, about 600 miles further than the Tour de France. Riders climb more than 200,000 ft. along the route, the equivalent of climbing from sea level to the summit of Mt. Everest nearly seven times back to back. The route's surface can be anything from benign pavement to the most remote, unmaintained trail, which could be covered in snow, a scree field, or littered with giant trees that have fallen or been pushed by avalanche across the trail.

And then there is the support, or lack of it. In professional races, like the Tour de France, riders are followed by team cars which carry food, water, tools, mechanics, and even extra bikes to keep the racers rolling. At the end of each day's stage, riders board a cushy team bus and are whisked in comfort to a hotel where the team's chef prepares gourmet meals.

In the Tour Divide (TD) each rider is his or her own support team. If a rider's bike breaks down on some godforsaken, wind-blown pass fifteen miles from the next town, she either fixes it herself or walks. If a rider gets hungry, she shops in the next trail town convenience store and scavenges what's available. If a rider gets tired, she tries to find a flat spot to pitch a tent. If a rider runs out of water...no, a racer had better never run out of water in the desert. The bottom line is if a person decides to take part in this race, she will do it alone. She will ride it alone, she will suffer alone, she will finish alone.

That is, if she finishes. The difficulty of this race, the physical and emotional toll it demands, is so great only about 5 out of every 10 people finish it. Nobody who tries a race this grueling does it on a whim.

Everyone who starts in Banff is an incredibly fit, motivated athlete. And then there was me, Grace, a petite, blonde, fifty-seven-year-old seamstress from Huntsville, Alabama. I was no stranger to challenge, but I had never attempted anything as remotely daunting as this. And unlike the other 132 racers lining up at the starting line, I would be carrying a passenger. This passenger's name was Multiple Sclerosis (MS). If I were to make it to the Mexican border, MS would be coming along for the ride. It was not a model travel companion. I had Relapsing Remitting MS, which attacked my central nervous system without warning, fogging my mind, impairing my vision, and squeezing the strength and coordination from my legs. An assault from MS combined with the rigors of a multi-week ride could be a one-two punch that might knock me out of the race.

Chapter 1

*One important key to success is self-confidence.
An important key to self-confidence is preparation.*
-Arthur Ashe

Preparation depends on control. When I decided in September 2017 to race the 2018 Tour Divide, I embarked on a mission to control every aspect of preparation and thus the race itself. I had nine months to get ready. *Nine months to deliver this baby.* Unlike having a real baby, though, which basically assembles itself, the success of this venture would be all on me. That was all right. I liked being in charge.

I became Ahab and the Tour Divide was my Moby Dick. In order to slay this beast, I had to develop a plan. First, I took stock of my current status. I had a few things going for me. I was already in good shape, my technical skill at riding a mountain bike was highly developed, and I had experience doing multi-day events.

The holes in my readiness, on the other hand, were gaping. Even my high level of base fitness would be nowhere near what it would need to be to tackle the mammoth distance of the TD. That part would be relatively easy to fix. I would use TITS to build my fitness. TITS stands for *Time In The Saddle,* in case anyone reading this thought it meant something more…titillating. In other words, I would just put my head down and ride. And ride. And ride some more.

It was the mysterious parts of the TD that took most of my attention. I had never "bikepacked" before. Bikepacking is just what it sounds like, backpacking on a bike. This was a whole new world. The questions and what-ifs were endless.

What do I need to maintain my fitness, health, and motivation for weeks?

How much food do I carry? How much water?

What is essential? What luxury will be essential to me?

How much weight can I carry? How much should I carry?

...and on and on.

For answers to these questions, I consulted my friend and backpacking guru, Dawson Wheeler. Dawson is an outdoors savant, having traveled both the Tour Divide and the Appalachian Trail. He gave me a thorough course on the complexities and nuances of bikepacking. If you think sleeping in the woods should be an uncomplicated subject, go to an internet chat room and ask for pros and cons of hammock vs. tent sleeping, or quilt vs. sleeping bag. The passion and zealotry of opinions about camping stoves rival those of the most strident religion.

Dawson broke down the task into digestible bites. Backpacking and bikepacking are all about stripping survival down to its basic requirements: shelter, clothing, food, and water. Comfort is a luxury to be sacrificed at the altar of space and weight. Storage is severely limited, and therefore commands a premium. Every ounce carried takes precious, finite watts from the body's power plant, so weight of gear is always measured with squinting precision.

The choices made my head spin, so I tabled my pursuit of camping gear and focused on something I understood: bikes. I already had a mountain bike which was trail capable, but this event required something more specialized. The keys were simplicity, durability, and speed. A bike with shock-absorbing suspension would be nice on a bumpy trail, but sluggish and bouncy on smooth road. Also, a failure of the suspension system would not be worth the extra comfort. The added weight of shocks was also a no-no, and I needed something that could hold a load of gear and retain its ride quality.

I had my eye on a bike called the Salsa Cutthroat. Despite its violent-sounding name, the bike is named for the official fish of every state through which the Tour Divide travels. In fact, the bike was specifically designed for the TD; it is a load-hauling, trail-tracking, long-distance race machine. It was perfect, but excellence comes at a price. In this case, the price was $2,500. I would have to write a grant proposal to the Challenged Athletes Foundation (CAF) for that kind of cheddar. The CAF was set up to help amputees stay active, but had expanded to assist those suffering from so-called 'silent diseases.' MS qualifies as silent, preferring to do its dirty work under cover of an unaffected exterior. One annoying thing that every MS patient hears is "...but you look so normal." If they only knew the devastation this evil disease caused inside.

I was humbled and thankful for CAF. They had contributed to my racing in the past, and I hoped they would help again. I added the lengthy grant-writing process to my ever-growing to-do list.

Autumn in the southeastern U.S. is an ephemeral burst of color and mild temperatures that crashes into a frigid yet snowless winter. I made steady progress throughout the season. I raced every chance I got. When I wasn't racing, I was training and researching. Control was not yet in my grasp, but I was gaining on it.

Piece by piece, gear choices were whittled down. I made pilgrimages from my home in Huntsville to big box outdoor stores in Chattanooga, Nashville, and Birmingham to "try on" sleeping bags and tents. I became familiar with arcane topics such as fill power rating, fabric denier ratings, and the nylon vs. polyester debate when talking about tent fly construction. I became so fluent in outdoors nerd jargon, I was able to slip references seamlessly into conversation. *"Well, sure, tariffs on China might negatively affect GDP and inflation, but what do you think about the cost-to-bulk ratio of 650FP down vs. 800FP?"* Or, *"Oh yeah, with the recent trades, I think the Broncos could win the championship this year, but how about Tentco's decision to use 30D nylon ripstop for their tent floors? I would've gone with 40D."*

Winter soon became spring. Redbuds and Dogwoods burst with pink and white flowers, the first trees to wake from the season of hibernation. I had not hibernated, but worked like a beaver to get ready. Dawson had given me homework assignments to simulate race conditions. I was tasked to set up my tent at night in the rain (didn't do it); load my bike with all my gear and do as many shakedown rides as I could; and shop for food at a gas station since that would be the only food available at times. I felt like I had been studying for a very long time, for a very big test. Study time was almost over. By the middle of May, I was riding 24 hours every week. I wasn't sure if my legs were ready for the TD, but my butt surely was.

In early June, I shipped my new Salsa Cutthroat to Canada and boarded a plane to follow it. I was proud of the effort I had put in to get ready. Everything unfolded according to plan. I had control. All my training, all my research, all my purchases had led to this moment. I was going to kill this race and leave MS in the dust.

Chapter 2

The geologic activity that builds mountain ranges is a slow, yet irresistible, force that creates the world's most beautiful scenery. I have never been anywhere this is more evident than in Banff, Canada. The beauty here is not only the product of the creative power of mountain building, but also its opposite, the destructive pressure of erosion. Once the mountain is fully grown, the patient and inexhaustible power of water, wind, and sun chip and scour the mountain until nothing but dust is left. The great glaciers above Banff are doing their part, grinding the sandstone into a fine rock flour which is carried down the slopes into the alpine lakes of the area. This flour is so finely ground and so uniformly shaped, it stays suspended in the lake for an unusually long time. This suspension catches sunlight at just the right wavelength to turn the lakes electric shades of turquoise and aquamarine. As I stared at the hypnotizing water of Lake Louise I realized that in opposition there is balance, and in balance, beauty.

I took some time, before the chaos began, to breathe and recollect the episodes and events that had led me to this moment. In a way, it had been like the processes that have created these mountains, both the building up and the tearing down. There had been plenty of destructive events along the way, but they had not destroyed me. In fact, the obstacles I had weathered, like MS, the death of my father, and divorce, had shaped my life into something uniquely mine. There had not always been balance in my life, but it always returned...and if it didn't, I pulled and pushed and kicked until I got it back where I wanted it.

On the other hand, I had never tried anything nearly as difficult as the Tour Divide. It would take everything I had to give for days, no, weeks on end. For all the bravado I exuded when talking to others, I wondered if, at last, I had gotten into something that bravery alone couldn't conquer. This was no time for doubt. I banished the thought and returned to my default setting; hubris.

The bike was retrieved from shipping and reassembled. Bags were packed and loaded. Checklists were checked and re-checked. Everything was going according to my ironclad plan except one thing. When I made it to Banff, a bothersome sore throat materialized out of thin air and a lymph node under my chin was swollen to the size of a grape. I did not count on sickness intruding on my race, and did not have time for it. I had a little less than forty-eight hours to kick whatever was testing my immune system, and it would be kicked.

As I crawled into bed, I threatened whatever was trying to put a kink in my plan.

I will kill you, little bug. I will find a way.
Find a way.

CHAPTER 3

The scratchy throat intensified overnight. I was officially on my way to being sick, which was not exactly an auspicious way to start a 2,700-mile race.

I have a term for the inconveniences that conspire to derail me from my goals. I call them border bullies; bullies that would keep me inside the borders where conventional thinking says I belong, like, "middle aged ladies with chronic diseases should be shopping and eating kale salads and going to yoga class." Well, I don't like bullies and I don't like borders. The next day was the day I had trained nine months for, and I wasn't about to miss it. I made my way to a walk-in clinic to get some help. Help was delivered to my backside via large-bore needles full of steroids and antibiotics. I went back to the motel to sleep and shake off the bug that was trying to be a border bully. I fully expected to wake the next morning without any trace of the threatening sickness.

That didn't happen. Apparently, the bugs were slow to obey. I awakened on race day with my throat on fire and a slight fever.

Okay, little bacteria, so that's how it's going to be, huh?

Most people would have said I had a choice to make. I could persevere or quit. Quitting wasn't an option. I had been training for months and preparing for years—really my whole life—for this moment. My destiny lay somewhere south of me on a dusty road and I had to find it, sick or not.

With nothing to do but push onward, I got dressed and strapped the last of my gear to my bike. The last things I put on were my big bag of food and my beloved flip flops; ugly, soot black sandals which would be the only footwear I would possess besides my riding shoes. Bike shoes have a large cleat that sticks out the bottom of the shoe and locks in to the pedal. It is very efficient for riding, but hilariously awkward to walk in. I imagined the best part of each day on the Tour would be the moment I removed my riding shoes and put on the flip flops. I carefully strapped the shoes and the big bag of food on top of my seat bag, which is the big bag that hangs from the saddle and is perched above the back tire.

My bag of food was ludicrously big. I had stuffed it with every kind of grab-and-go food imaginable, including trail mix, gummy bears, performance bars, and Snickers. As this was a race, I wanted to be as light as possible and also have quick access, so I had stripped everything of its wrapper, jammed each type of food into its own Ziploc bag, and dumped everything into the big, waterproof bag. It weighed five pounds. FIVE POUNDS.

I looked at the loaded bike. Everything that would sustain me and propel me for the next few weeks—my clothing, my shelter, my food, my transportation, my communication—was contained in this ridiculously small package. The simplicity was liberating and a little frightening.

What if I need something I don't have?

Too late now. I pedaled the mile from my hotel to the starting line. Most of the racers were already assembled for the Grand Depart. It was a little bit of a misnomer calling it the Grand Depart, which brings to mind throngs of flag-waving, cheering spectators lining the closed streets, as brightly-clad racers tear through the middle of town. It wasn't like that at all. First of all, the racers look like dirtbag cross-country touring riders. Second, it's an amateur and (I'm being generous here) obscure race. Most dedicated cyclists haven't even heard of the Tour Divide, much less your average Banff vacationer. I imagine the tourists were probably a little confused at the incongruous spectacle of 132 cyclists lined up for what looked like a race, but all riding bikes loaded down with touring gear.

A local man named Crazy Larry was the "official" starter for this very unofficial race. Someone uninitiated in the world of unsupported, long-distance bike racing would mistake Crazy

Larry for a real TD rider, but several pieces of his gear betrayed him. First, he was wearing a dayglo yellow safety vest. Where we were going, the most likely thing to run over a rider would be a wild animal, so a safety vest would probably be superfluous. Second, he had multiple plastic shopping bags dangling from his handlebars, which no serious racer would ever do. Crazy Larry was eccentric, but he was a unique character and a well-loved fixture of the TD. He gave a rousing, rambling speech and sent us on our way. Despite the ominous feeling that I would end this day much sicker, possibly pushing myself into an early exit out of the race, I felt the elation of beginning a new journey and the excitement of all the adventures to be uncovered on the road stretched out before me.

CHAPTER 4

Because of the cold, flu, or whatever the hell was plaguing me, I modified my plan for the day. I had originally planned on spending the first night of the race in my tent somewhere in the great Canadian wilderness, but the thought of having a real bed, in a real room, sounded more recuperative, so I decided to push myself to the town of Elkford, the first town I would come to after leaving Banff. One small detail: Elkford is 103 miles from Banff with one big uphill climb to cross the Divide and innumerable smaller hills to traverse. It would have been a big day for a healthy rider. As for a sick fifty-seven-year-old woman with MS...well, we would see.

The day was picture-perfect, sunny but absent the omnipresent humidity I am used to in the south. It was a little weird starting in a bustling town like Banff, riding in the midst of churning traffic, past the stately Fairmont Banff Springs Hotel, knowing that within a few minutes civilization as most of us know it, with cars, people, and stores, would vanish like a hazy dream, leaving only deserted, dusty roads, wild animals, and forlorn, forgotten towns. And mountains. Mile after mile of beguiling, dangerous mountains.

Minutes came and went. Banff came and went. And there it was, the boundless Rocky Mountain wilderness which would swallow me for days. How many days, I did not know. I did the only thing I could. I plunged in and pedaled on.

The day's ride unfolded as well as I could've hoped given my weakened state. The Spray River Trail which took us out of Banff, immersed riders in the stunning beauty of Kananaskis Country, or "K-Country" as the locals call it, a line of sparkling national and regional mountain parks that have been called "the string of pearls."

When I was very young, way before cycling became my passion, I loved to play with dolls. I would dress and undress them, fascinated by the combinations of colors, shapes and textures. My favorite piece was a fake pearl necklace with which I would accessorize every outfit, no matter how malapropos. One day, Daddy took notice.

"Pearls with a bathing suit, huh? She's going to be the most fashionable girl at the pool."

I laughed. "I think they look pretty."

"They are," he said. "One day, when you are grown up, I will get you a necklace just like that."

My daddy was my world. My first friend, my hero. Daddy was a college band director and would sometimes take me to his rehearsals. When he saw me admiring the glamorous majorettes, he would take me aside and warn that I would never be allowed to be one. I didn't question his wisdom when I was five, but for years I wondered what dark magic the twirlers possessed that made them so dangerous.

When daddy stood on the podium and controlled the musicians with a wave of his baton, he was elevated to god status. I wanted to be near this deity who created music with a flick of his wrist, so I stood at his feet and looked up in awe. More than once, he hit me accidentally with a dramatic downstroke, sending waves of titters through the band and breaking the spell.

"Dammit, Gracie!" he would sputter. He said it often enough that Dammitgracie became my nickname to the band. I still use the moniker on my blog and email address.

Daddy was multi-talented. Skilled not just in the cerebral world of music, but also adept in the practical matters of life. He could build houses and repair cars just like any Joe Sixpack. He was an adventurer and an outdoorsman as well. He seemed to know everything, and I worshipped him for it.

My mother arced a wide orbit around normalcy, so Daddy was also my lifeline to sanity. Sadly, he was gone with the marching band or touring with his own jazz band much of the time, leaving me to figure out life mostly on my own. His absence reinforced my impression of him as a deity, the benefactor who remained mysterious and mostly inaccessible. As I grew older and became engulfed by the flames of adolescence, I slipped further from him and into my own ego.

Then, when I was seventeen, he was diagnosed with advanced melanoma. I watched in horror and confusion as he withered; too scared to talk to him, too scared to say something stupid and make his illness worse. His polyester suit, which had been filled out with typical middle age padding, began to droop from his frame like it was hung on a coat hanger. I began to fear what life would look like without my daddy. He had been such a kind, stabilizing presence, soothing me when Mama unsettled me with her bizarre behavior. I told a friend I would be up shit creek without my Daddy. I was lost in fear, coping the only way I knew how, by denying the inevitable until it came to pass.

Daddy died when I was eighteen, less than a year after his diagnosis. I was right on the threshold of adulthood and independence, with a mother who was only a brief acquaintance of reality, and no clue how I was going to make it on my own. The one connection I had to conventionality was Daddy, and he was gone forever. Within a few months, Mama sold his instruments and our little vacation cottage on the river, wiping away every tangible connection to his life, short-circuiting the grieving process and tearing me apart. The shock and fear resonated through the decades. I can still feel the echoes of it today.

For the next few years, I was lost. Not knowing how to mourn properly, I suppressed the pain. The void left by Daddy's absence was filled by the dark shadow of an MS diagnosis six months after his death. I mostly ignored that too as I tried on different identities; party girl, college student, girlfriend, wife. I searched the options at hand, which were fairly limited for a southern girl in the early eighties.

On my 21st birthday, Mama threw a petite, wrapped gift box at me. It was an odd gesture for a woman who had never given me a wrapped gift in my whole life. I opened the box and read the brief card scratched in familiar handwriting.

Happy birthday, Grace. Love, Daddy.

I pulled a string of pearls from the box. He remembered.

I searched for many more years to find who I was, but I would never forget one timeless identity. I would always be Daddy's girl.

I wheezed my way through the magical wilderness, noticeably handicapped by the infection. The trail was sometimes gravel road, sometimes swoopy singletrack. I love the roller-coaster sensation of swoopy singletrack, but it's not quite the same thrill on a fifty-five -pound touring bike that it is on a nimble mountain bike.

The extra weight meant that I would be pushing my bike up hills I would normally ride. I was also having a small issue with my seat bag rubbing against the tire with each dip in the trail, but it felt so exhilarating to finally be racing, I ignored it for a while. When I stopped to refill my water bladder, I decided to take a look at the offending bag.

Oh shit, my flip flops are gone!

One of my few comfort items, my beloved flip flops, were now sitting all alone somewhere in the Canadian wilderness. I thought about going to find them for a moment, then realized the folly of turning back. They could be anywhere along the 50 miles I had ridden. I mourned the loss for a few minutes and cursed my foolish placement of the shoes on the seat bag. Then I imagined a Grizzly bear picking them up and trying them on.

If Mr. Grizz comes sauntering into my campsite wearing my flip flops, there's going to be a fight.

As I was finishing my adjustments, a fellow racer rolled up to me. He was carrying one—ONE—of my flip flops.

"Is this yours?" he asked. "I found it about five miles back."

Now, if he had been carrying two, I would have swallowed my pride and admitted my stupidity, but I wasn't about to fall on my sword for one worthless shoe.

"Nope, not mine. Must belong to some dummy up ahead. What a dork, haha."

He rode off with my flip flop, looking for the dummy up ahead. Meanwhile, the dork who lost the flip flops refilled her water bladder and continued south. As I rode, the tightness in my chest intensified just as I was starting the biggest challenge of the day—the first crossing of the Continental Divide over the 6,400 ft. Elk Pass.

Climbing a mountain on a bike divides cyclists into two distinct camps. They either love it or hate it. Generally speaking, skinny little dudes and girls often profess their love for it, while heavier riders tend to hate it for obvious reasons. I'm a skinny little girl so I usually love it, but on this day, I had gained 50 pounds. It didn't matter that the weight was on the bike and not on me. Gravity does not discriminate. It made a hard climb excruciatingly hard.

I pushed, I sweated, I wheezed, I cursed. Finally, after an hour of non-stop effort, I reached the top of the gap.

Great, I panted, *only 31 more gaps to go.*

At the top, I ran into a group of riders taking a break. One rider named George heard my labored breathing and handed me his albuterol inhaler.

"Here ya go. Have a suck on that."

I'm not in the habit of accepting drugs from strangers, but two puffs of the inhaler and I could feel my lungs opening. I took a moment to appreciate the expansive, postcard-worthy view and the renewed flow of oxygen into my lungs.

Thirty miles to Elkford, a bed, and rest. I was going to make it.

CHAPTER 5

When I woke up the next morning, it was nearly noon. I was in a motel room, disoriented, and very sick. The last eighteen hours were hazy. I remember arriving in Elkford and having dinner with my "drug dealer" George and his riding partner Sam. They offered to give me a bed in their room. I also vaguely remembered the sound of them shuffling around the room gathering their things. It turned out they left at 4 a.m. to get a jump on the day and left me there to sleep.

The 103-mile effort from Banff to Elkford had left me depleted, and now I was going to pay for it with a lost day. It was only the second day, so all the racers, even the ones who didn't make it to Elkford yesterday, would be rolling through town and leaving me behind. If I hadn't been so sick, this thought would have panicked me. Thankfully, I was too tired for self-recrimination, so I went back to bed. I spent the day sleeping and drinking water. In the evening, I was still tired, so I called my coach, Kym, for advice. Kym, bless her heart, could tell I was still running on fumes and told me to stay put for another day. Without her direction, I would have succumbed to my natural inclination to play through the pain, saddled up and ridden on Day Three, and ended up withdrawing from the race from exhaustion. In addition to *Find a way,* one of my other mantras is *Eyes on the prize.* Sometimes my single-minded focus creates a blind spot to more strategic thinking. I'm a bull—a 110-pound bull—but a bull nonetheless, always charging ahead. It was good to have a cooler head guiding me when I needed it most. I obeyed and went back to sleep.

My life originated in the eastern U.S., where there is no such thing as a 'new' town. Elkford, British Columbia is just that, a new town. It was incorporated in 1971 to serve the massive open pit coal mine that had opened on the nearby Fording River in the late sixties. As has always been the case, new industry in remote locations, whether it was the coal boom in Appalachia or the gold rush in California, attracts the ambitious and the desperate, who leave their familiar, unsatisfactory life to hack out a better life in an unknown, often inhospitable country.

The pull of opportunity reaches across cultural, ethnic, and even linguistic boundaries. Boom towns that spring up around mineral extraction industries often become mini melting pots, with little towns boasting an ethnic and racial diversity unexpected in such small and remote places. Elkford is such a town. With a population of barely 2,500, it nevertheless attracted a Chinese family of entrepreneurs who ran the Elkford Motor Lodge where I was impatiently recuperating. Despite the language barrier, I managed to communicate with the family. It's funny, we come from two cultures that couldn't be more dissimilar, yet we both spoke the basic human language, which is body language. The family could tell I was sick and they displayed compassion to the point of mothering me, which was such a touching gesture. Once when I was sitting in the small café attached to the motel, I ordered coffee and water. The waitress, who also doubled as the housekeeper, said in her heavily accented, broken English, "You no need water, you need hot tea and sweet-sour soup." I was too tired to argue. I nodded my head weakly and she disappeared into the kitchen, and returned with a steaming tray. She was right. Like liquid strength, the soup and tea revived me. It was like magic.

Trail Magic.

Trail Magic is a term most likely originated on the Appalachian Trail, where long distance hikers are periodically and unexpectedly offered gifts of food, supplies, or a ride to a resupply town which might be miles off the trail. The Appalachian Trail Conservancy defines it as "an unexpected act of kindness that lifts a hiker's spirits and inspires awe or gratitude." Trail Magic has spread to all the long-distance hiking trails in the U.S. and has even made its way to the Tour Divide. The providers of Trail Magic are called, appropriately, Trail Angels. The riders speak of both Magic and Angels reverently. The lonely world of the TD racer is one where even the strongest athletes often walk a tightrope of emotion, and even the slightest gust of despair can blow a competitor right out of the race. An act of kindness by a Trail Angel may be the difference between quitting or continuing.

The little Chinese lady was my first Trail Angel. She was concerned for me even though she didn't have to be. Though we did not share a common spoken language, she gifted me in a way that transcended such trivial, earthly barriers. We were bonded by our shared humanity and the simple, yet profound act of giving and receiving. It was the first time on the race in which I felt such a powerful combination of awe and gratitude. I hoped it would not be the last.

CHAPTER 6

Day 4 of the Tour Divide broke across the ridgeline of the Great Divide in waves of glorious sunshine. It was to be my second start of this great undertaking and I could hear heavenly voices cascading down the mountain as I threw a leg over the bike and triumphantly rode out of town.

Yeah, not so much.

It was true that I was basically starting over, but there were no hallelujah choruses serenading me. In fact, I had a strong feeling of dread and nervousness that started the night before when I knew I would be rejoining the race on this day. It was a strange dichotomy. On one hand, I was miserable knowing the race had passed me by and I couldn't wait to get back in the game. On the other hand, there was this weird feeling of comfort that had grown in me while I was at the motel. There were no wrong turns to be taken there, no breakdowns in the middle of nowhere to deal with, no physical discomfort to bear, and no bears to cause me discomfort...or death.

Maybe I should get a job at the motel and stay here forever.

No. Whatever my fears were, it was time to move on and face them. My life passed through Elkford, but it didn't belong in Elkford. My life belonged to the trail; the one that stretched for the next 2,600 miles, and the next trail after that, and the one after that. My best life was nomadic, not stationary.

As I put the remaining gear on the bike (including the ludicrous bag of food) I felt a tug on my jersey. My little Chinese grandma was standing there, gesturing to me that she wanted a picture. I hugged her tightly while her husband took a picture of us. I then threw a leg over my bike and rode out of town, maybe not triumphantly as I had fantasized, but more determined than ever.

As I rode, I took a mental inventory to get to the root of what was bothering me. In addition to MS, I struggle with anxiety and depression. I have discovered the best cure for anxiety is to break the big black cloud of doom down into its essence and, once identified, to name it and tame it. This particular cloud had many roots, mostly under the heading of "what if."

What if my GPS dies and I get lost, what if I wreck and break it, what if I loaded the wrong course, and the biggest "what if" of all; *what if I meet a bear?*

The bears. Dear God, the effing bears. The section I would be riding on this day was the start of the unofficially, but forebodingly, named "Grizzly Bear Highway," where, according to official people who keep such statistics, you'll find the largest population of inland Grizzlies in North America. It was one thing to run this gauntlet in the relative safety of a thinly-stretched pack of racers, but they were all two days ahead of me. I would be facing this border bully by myself. I looked at the canister of bear spray banging against my handlebar bag and wondered if it would be enough to save my life. Hopefully I wouldn't have to find out.

One of the first written accounts of *Ursus horribilis*, better known as the Grizzly bear, came from the journals of Lewis and Clark as they made their way across the Continental Divide in 1805. These hardened, fearless men with multiple weapons had scoffed at the stories the Shoshones had told of the "white bear." Merriwether Lewis even boasted in his journal "...in the hands of skillful riflemen they are by no means as formidable or dangerous as they have been represented."

Over the next few weeks, the members of the Corps of Discovery were attacked and harassed multiple times by huge, 500 to 600-pound Grizzlies. Each time, the animal displayed a ferocity and resistance to bullets that nearly cost several men their lives, including Lewis, who once had to run into a frigid, chest-deep river to escape a murderous bear. These episodes instilled in them a deep respect for this king of the mountains. After the encounters, Lewis deadpanned in his journal "This bear being so hard to die rather intimidates us all. I must confess that I do not like the gentleman..."

Along with the thought of bears, another source of my anxiety wasn't a "what-if" like a bear encounter that may never happen, but a full-blown "this is happening and it's going to suck." "This" was the section of the race that would take us over the infamous Koko Claims trail. Matthew Lee, TD race director and legendary six-time TD winner, notified the racers back in the winter that this year's race would include the "monster 2.5-hour hike-a-bike between Elkford and Fernie." I snorted at his 2.5-hour estimate.

Yeah, right, 2.5 hours if you are under 35 and have been racing at a pro level for, like, forever.

I didn't have to spend much mental energy wondering exactly how hard the climb was going to be as it more or less started right outside of Elkford. As I climbed up the gravel road toward the trail, I remembered some intel a previous TD racer had shared with me about the descent of Koko Claims. He said that much of it was un-rideable (these words are often taken by experienced mountain bikers as a challenge) and contained many creek crossings, some deep, cold, and fast. Drowning and hypothermia are no joke in the wilderness, but I tried to laugh off the danger by imagining myself trying to ford a knee-deep, glacial creek while my fifty-five-pound bike caught water like a sail and flushed me down a continent-sized water slide all the way to the Gulf of Mexico...or the Pacific. I wasn't sure which side of the divide I was on.

In the nine months I had spent preparing for this adventure, I sought out previous racers for their advice. All gave me excellent tips, but one thing that was never mentioned was the cast of characters I would meet along the trail. Of course, everybody knows and mentions Crazy Larry because he is a fixture in

Banff. But no two people ever have the exact same race, so they don't run across the same strangers and their stories don't grow into legend. The people we meet are the result of the alchemy of circumstance and timing. My Chinese grandma was one of these unique encounters, born of illness and empathy. I was about to have another. This one wouldn't be so...um...normal.

Around hour number four of my 2.5-hour climb, I was noticing the thickness of the fir and spruce trees and wondering how many Grizzlies were hiding in there, when I rounded a turn and saw a rider up ahead, standing next to his bike.

I was so excited to see another human being, I shouted, "Hey, TD rider!" Admittedly, this was an assumption since TD racers don't display race numbers or any other accoutrements one would see in a normal, saner race. He could have been just a regular bikepacker out here on vacation, but I figured my guess had better than 50/50 odds of being correct. As I rolled up to him, I noticed a hilarious gash in his rain pants that traveled the entire length of his butt crack. (Thankfully, he had another layer between the ventilated rain pants and, well, you know...)

Curiously, he was holding several of his personal items; driver's license, credit cards, cash, passport, in one hand and a ball of twine in the other. I was reminded of Dawson's lessons about the value of packing light. A heavy and bulky ball of twine would have been way down the list of priorities for me. I decided to hold off on the judgement and put my best sorority girl/cheerleader foot forward. After all, this was a real live person! I was no longer alone! I was not hopelessly in last place!

"How are you?!" I gushed.

"Ah, not too good," came the glum reply.

He then told me his bizarre tale of getting lost for the LAST FOUR DAYS, which meant that he had been lost more or less since we left Banff. He had climbed Koko Claims once, only to be advised by his GPS that he was off course, so he backtracked all the way to Elkford to call Matthew Lee. Somewhere along his second trip up Koko Claims, he had lost his personal effects and had to backtrack again to retrieve them. When I found him, he had just gathered all his items and was about to tie them to his bike with the twine. Now, I freely admit I am not the all-knowing guru when it comes to bikepacking pro tips, but twine didn't seem to be the optimal material to secure items. In fact, it seemed downright dumb.

Despite my reservations about his navigational skills, packing savvy, and general sanity, I was so overjoyed to have company I overlooked the oddities of this man. (There is probably a personal safety lesson here: never let yourself become so isolated that you brush aside all red flags just to have companionship.) As it turns out, the man's eccentricities were harmless and he was a good guy. His name was Mark. Mark and I rode for a while before we came to the main course, Koko Claims. We dismounted and started to push. The trail was as ridiculous as advertised. Nearly vertical in places, the difficulty of the trail's steepness was matched by its surface, which resembled the rocky bottom of a dry streambed more than a trail. In some places, a frigid glacial stream would tumble across the trail and follow it for several hundred feet, completing the feeling that we were climbing a waterfall. My feet were wet and cold, the air temperature was in the mid-30s, and the misery of pushing a heavy bike was draining. But the fun wasn't over yet.

Before we reached the top of the climb, we came upon an obstacle that, if I didn't know better, I would have sworn had been erected by the race organizers to test the will of the racers. A wall some twenty feet high, made of broken trees, dirt, and rocks piled across the trail. This recent landslide had menacing splinters of tree trunks sticking out from its flanks like some medieval fortress.

Before tackling this beast, Mark and I sat down to have a snack. He began talking immediately.

"I'm riding for M.S."

"You're what?"

He explained that he was racing to raise funds for Multiple Sclerosis and he was one of the largest fundraisers in California. A smile crept across my face as I considered my response. Finally, I said, "Thank you."

"Come again?"

"Thank you. Because of people like you, the face of MS has changed radically since my diagnosis in 1980. Who knows, someday, maybe some bonehead with MS may be dumb enough to try the Tour Divide!"

We laughed, but he was floored. I think he had a moment of deep satisfaction when he realized the return on hundreds of hours he had invested in fighting MS came in the form of one old lady riding this stupid, maddening, and wonderful race with him.

We made it over the avalanche of fallen trees and debris and rode together for a little while, but it became evident Mark was not going to be able to match my pace. This was a race after all. We said adios and I rode on ahead, wondering how he was ever going to make it.

The downhill of Koko Claims was just as treacherous as the uphill, requiring me to walk much of it. Eventually I made it off the trail and back onto a fire road, which, after the rocks and steepness of Koko Claims, felt like gliding down the interstate.

I passed a collection of trashy-looking teepees and tents that looked like a homeless village or possibly some kind of cult. Thankfully it was deserted. Nevertheless, it weirded me out and I picked up the pace. Then I heard a noise that chilled me.

A car was coming up behind me. I thought of the most rational possibility why a car would be this far out in the boonies.

Oh no, the Homeless Teepee Murder Cult has a car and is coming to abduct me.

I tried to act casual, yet dangerous, as the car pulled up beside me. I imagined that the cult members in the car were sizing me up for a possible mark. The car slowed and I got ready to grab the bear spray. I looked at the occupants, expecting to see frightening, dirty mountain men. They were dirty but an otherwise friendly-looking man and woman. I decided they did not look like members of the Homeless Teepee Murder Cult. When they opened their mouth to speak, however, I realized I was dealing with something much more unexpected...they were French.

The pair was apparently dirtbagging it along the Canadian wilderness and flagged me down. The man said in his heavily accented, Pepe LePew English, "Your friend has crashed and hurt his shoulder."

I wanted to make sure they were talking about Mark, so I asked them if he had a big rip in the seat of his pants. They howled with laughter.

"Oui, oui! Ha-ha! Right down the crack!"

After sharing a good laugh, I asked how far back he was. They said about 20 miles.

Twenty miles?

I couldn't go that far back to check on him. I felt bad, but there was no way I could add forty miles to this day. I bid adieu to my French friends and continued on to Fernie, hoping the best for Mark, but feeling a little guilty.

CHAPTER 7

The next morning, I immensely enjoyed the buffet at the white tablecloth restaurant attached to the swanky hotel I had splurged for the night before. It was a bad financial decision, costing more than $200, but after the difficulty of the last few days, I decided I deserved a little pampering. I am a southern girl, after all, and even us dirtbag types enjoy a little finery every once in a while. In my defense, when I rolled into Fernie, I was exhausted. It had been a hard day on the bike and I still wasn't fully recovered from the crud that had dogged me since Banff. The thought of milled French soap, high thread count sheets, shampoo AND conditioner, and a blow dryer weakened my resolve to live like a hobo.

As I sat in the restaurant, I realized the fire in my belly was back. I was ready to get back out there and race! Finally! The mojo had returned! Stella got her groove back, and it was time to kick some butt! I chalked up my new enthusiasm to the $200 per night bed I slept in the night before, and rationalized that my ill-advised purchase was actually a wise investment in my health and wellbeing that would pay dividends as the weeks unfold.

Yeah, right.

But my hair *was* shiny and silky smooth.

It was another cool day in the mountains. My riding attire for this weather consisted of a wool base layer, jog bra, short sleeve jersey, buff, headband, arm and knee warmers, wool knee socks and gloves that were windproof and waterproof. The rest of my kit was not much more extensive. I had rain gear, a microfiber jacket with a hood, and 'town clothes,' which consisted of underwear, capri pants, and a shirt. That was my entire closet for the next few weeks. I appreciated the simplicity of my wardrobe immensely. With no choices to make about what to wear, my mind was uncluttered and freed of the stress and distractions that come from a focus on fashion. It was liberating, but I remember a time when I was quite the fashionista.

My other career, besides riding a bike nearly full time, was sewing. I came to be a seamstress at a very young age, and quite by accident. When I was in the second grade, Mama decided it would be fun to take a sewing class. Because Daddy was on the faculty at the university, family members could take classes for free. Daddy's schedule wouldn't allow him to babysit me while she was in class, and babysitters cost money she either didn't have or didn't want to spend, so she grudgingly took me along with her.

Thankfully, the teacher took a liking to me. She taught me basic hand stitches and gave me a project to do every class. By the end of the semester, I had progressed to the sewing machine and made a couple of outfits for my teddy bear and dolls.

Over Christmas break, I begged Mama to sign us up for Sewing 102. She did and I was able to continue my higher education at age eight! The teacher had me sew a skirt. I was so proud of the skirt and pleaded with Mama to let me wear it to school. She agreed, but only if I included a couple of accessories.

This would be a good time to admit that my mother was non-traditional. Looking back with the understanding of an adult, maybe crazy was a more accurate description. She was attractive, witty, and unfiltered. Oh, and an alcoholic. Though we lived in the Deep South city of Chattanooga, Tennessee, where conformity to social mores was enforced with an iron fist by the keepers of culture and the fossilized descendants of Sir Walter Scott's chivalrous fictions, Mama marched to her own drummer. I can almost see her with a cigarette dangling from her lips as she declared, "Well, the Junior League can kiss my ass."

Mama's additions to my outfit included a sixties flipped bob wig and go-go boots. The fact that the boots belonged to her and were about five sizes too big for me did not matter to her. In her defense though, she suggested that I take off the boots for recess. I imagine my teacher nearly wet her pants seeing an eight year-old go-go dancer come strutting into the classroom that day. I wish I had a picture of it.

Over the next few years, my sewing obsession continued. Mama would buy me all the fabric I wanted, but never clothes. Fortunately, I had a steady stream of hand-me-downs from family friends or Daddy's majorettes. I cut, altered, and sewed everything. I loved my funky clothes and felt proud knowing that I was creating something unique, like a piece of art that I could wear. Eventually, though, my non-conformist streak would be tamed by the very social enforcers that Mama despised, the kind of people who would frown upon a woman riding a bike alone in the wilderness, the kind of border bullies who took the caste system very seriously.

As I made my way out of Fernie, I stopped by a grocery store. I had not developed a rhythm yet in this whole bikepacking/ultra racing universe, and in no area was this more evident than my food. In a nutshell, I was consistently packing more food than I needed. I suppose it is a natural human tendency to hoard food when it's available, especially when thrust into an environment where you're not sure how much you need or when the next resupply opportunity will come. I repeated the rookie mistake several times before developing a sense of what I truly needed.

At the store, my crazy shopping spree included apple pie, cheese, a really long rope of salami, sourdough bread, Canadian Payday bars, and my favorite, Snickers. I probably added two more pounds to my already overweight Ludicrous Food Bag. I also continued to unwrap each food item (gotta save weight, you know) and cram similar food items into their own Ziploc bag. This would prove to be another rookie error discovered as I opened the bag to see my individual portions had melted together and hardened into an unbreakable conglomerate. Eating it was an unladylike affair of holding the head-sized food mound with both hands while gnawing at it like a beaver on a tree trunk.

I thought I had been wise by getting up at 6 a.m. to get a jump on the day. However, I spent a stupid amount of time in the grocery store (three hours) and didn't leave town until late morning. Good thing the daylight lasted until about 10 p.m. As I rode through town, I saw three bikepackers ahead of me.

TD riders!

I stomped on the pedals to catch them. Alas, they were not racers, but just three friends out for a leisurely week of riding. I remained in next-to-last place, assuming Mark didn't abandon the race after his wreck.

My goal was to reach Butts Cabin, fifty miles deep in the Flathead National Park Preserve. The cabin is free to all and maintained by the park department. The views along this section were stunning; wide valleys framed by the snow-capped peaks of the Divide. It was also known as "The Grizzliest place in North America" for having the highest density of bears on the continent. If that wasn't enough, there are lots of other predators in the area. A tourism website called Crown of the Continent announces rather nonchalantly, "in addition to dense populations of Grizzly bears and cougars, this is the first place that wolves migrated to after a fifty-year absence."

Wait a minute. Bears, cougars AND wolves? A few jellyfish at the beach will send swimmers scrambling out of the water like it's a scene from *Jaws*, but a forest full of big, fast, and powerful apex predators is considered a selling point by the tourism board. Now I knew how Dorothy felt in the Wizard of Oz.

Wolves, and cougars, and bears, oh my.

In my preparation for the TD, I paid special attention to the lessons on being bear aware. It was bear springtime; they were getting up from their long winter slumber, they were very hungry, and they were raising babies. This made for a very grumpy bear and the last thing I wanted to do was to startle a grumpy bear. I had attached a device called a bear bell to my handlebar bag (named delightfully by the manufacturer *The Sweet Roll*). The bell came with a kill switch, which was a magnet that would keep it from ringing. Because of the rough terrain I was riding, the kill switch kept falling onto the bell, silencing it. I was so nervous about running up on a bear because he couldn't hear my bell, I finally cut the magnet off the bell. The bell then rang constantly, which was annoying, but was a small price to pay for a little peace of mind. I was aware of the preposterous fact that my primary defense against this 600-lb monster was a bicycle bell.

I also used my voice to warn any nearby bears, cougars, or wolves of my presence. I sang, which, considering the quality of my singing voice (somewhere between atrocious and abysmal) constituted a significant weapon in my efforts to deter any would-be attacker. I also repeated Mother Goose rhymes as loud as I could, which was not very loud because of my lingering infection.

> *Hey diddle diddle, the bear and the fiddle*
> *The cougar jumped over the moon*
> *The little wolf laughed to see such a sight*
> *And Grace pedaled her ass off and got the hell out of there*

A few days before I left my home in Huntsville, Alabama to make my way west for the TD, I called my buddy, 2013 TD finisher Scott Thigpen. Scott was the first finisher from Alabama. I hoped to be the second, and the first finisher with MS. I confided my fears about the bears to Scott. He calmed me by saying not to be so concerned about the Grizzlies, "unless you are wrapped in bacon." I shared a laugh with Scott over the thought of being an appetizer on the Grizzly Diner's menu.

Try our new bacon-wrapped white girl!

His assurances and humor helped me be at peace a little bit about the bears, at least until I actually got out there amongst the bears.

I made it to Butts Cabin about 3:30 in the afternoon. The cabin was occupied by four hunters with their camo, guns, and ATVs. Seeing as the cabin was full and I still had about five more hours of daylight, I decided to press on 27 more miles to Wigwam campground. The day was so bluebird perfect, the views so spectacular, I even forgot about the bears for a while.

My reverie was broken by a logging truck which flew by and covered me in dust. Then came another. And another. The drivers were obviously used to seeing cyclists on this road, for they gave little space and didn't bother to slow down. I was reminded of my years of riding on the roads in Alabama. If one wants to be a road cyclist there, she must be willing to endure the disrespect and danger created by drivers who can't stand sharing the road with cyclists. I spent many tense hours on the roads there and was exposed to some of the most hateful, impatient drivers. Now, here I was, thousands of miles from home, in one of the most remote places on the continent, and felt that same stress I did when I was between a pickup truck driver and Walmart...or a soccer mom and Target...or a retiree and the golf course...or pick your favorite cyclist-hating stereotype, there are plenty to choose from.

I could hear another truck shifting gears in the distance behind me. I pulled my buff over my face to prepare for a fresh coating of dust. To my surprise, the driver slowed as he approached. As he came alongside me, he rolled down his window. I was bracing for some variation of, "Hey, you stupid biker, get off the road." He shouted over the soft roar of the engine.

"Hey, great job, are you in the Tour Divide race?"

I pulled down my buff and smiled. "Yes I am, probably in last place." I said the words with a self-deprecating chuckle, but this was a fact which stung my pride.

He laughed. "Well, you are doing great! I bet you are hungry. Would you like some homemade fried chicken and a candy bar?"

Trail Magic struck again! "Yes! I am starving for real food!"

He gave me the food and disappeared. I can't overstate the effect that this simple act of sharing had on my spirits. I rode the rest of the way to Wigwam on an energy source that seemed outside my body. Maybe it was magic.

I made it to Wigwam as the daylight was ebbing into the infinite blackness of the wilderness night. I pulled out the rest of my fried chicken and ate it far away from my campsite, just as my backwoods guru, Dawson, had advised. The idea is that you want to keep the scent of food far away from your sleeping area. As I gnawed on the chicken, I scanned the area for a suitable tree limb from which to hang my food bag.

I saw a limb with two crows sitting on it.

"Hello, John. Hello, Mikey," I said.

The limb was about twenty feet above ground, high enough to flummox even the tallest bear. I walked over to the tree to begin the business of hanging the bag. The crows moved to an adjacent tree to watch the show, which proved to be more difficult and hilarious than I expected. I tied one end of the rope to the food bag, and the other end to a baseball-sized rock. So far, so good. Now I just had to throw the rock over the limb, then hoist the bag up and tie it off.

This would be a good time to admit that I suck at throwing anything. There I was, still in my riding clothes, including my helmet, trying again and again to get the blasted rock over the limb. Overhand. Underhand. On one of my tries, I managed to hit the limb with my rock, only to have it ricochet, come straight down, and hit me in the head. I was very glad I was wearing my helmet. Without it I might have spent the night knocked out cold right next to my still-unhung food bag. In the bear world, they probably call this a two-for-one special.

CHAPTER 8

Despite my hilarious ineptitude, I managed to hang my bear bag the night before. I woke up the next morning with the sun streaming in my tent, and my bear bag was still hanging in the tree.

Yay for Gracie the backwoods woman!

Today would be a big day. I would cross the border and be back in the USA. However, before I would be reunited with my homeland, I would have some big challenges to face, including a legendary obstacle known simply as "The Wall."

The first twenty miles of the ride was a scenic cruise along the Wigwam river, interrupted by the occasional logging truck spewing road dust. There were no Angels bearing fried chicken today. After twelve miles or so, I turned off the road and followed a riverside trail. Eventually, the trail left the river and started ascending. I rounded a bend and there it was. The Wall.

A trail feature has never had a blander—or more accurate—name. It looked to be about a quarter mile of bushwhacking, vertical hell with loose rocks, roots, mud, ruts, and running water. TD vets suggested that I take off my bags, hike them up to the top, then return to the bottom to retrieve the bike. So, I removed my Sweet Roll, seat bag, and the Ludicrous Food Bag and trudged up the hill. If the trail had been any steeper, I would have needed crampons and an ice axe. Once reaching the top, I dropped the bags and returned for the hard part. Anyone who has pushed a bike up a hill knows that it is an ungainly activity. Throw in a slippery, super steep surface, and I might as well have been rolling a boulder uphill.

Grace and Jill went up the hill to fetch a pail of water
Grace came down wearing a frown...

...because she had to push her bike back up that friggin' hill

Having scaled the wall, I took a lunch break. After lunch, it was off to find America. My climbing wasn't over. The five-mile climb up to 6,300 ft. Galton Pass took hours. The ride downhill was exhilarating and included some of the oddest road obstacles I had encountered—cows! Free range Hereford cows were all over the road and didn't seem to mind me weaving in and out amongst them. It was such a feeling of freedom. My bike weaved and dipped like a magic carpet beneath me, the sun was shining, and I was sailing on the breeze. As I descended further, the valley opened up before me. It contained fields and houses.

Civilization.

America.

Home.

I can't explain why I felt such a rush of emotion as I approached the border. It's not like I had spent years away in some kind of concentration camp. It was just Canada, and I had only been gone for a few days. And, truth be told, I had never lived a day of my life within a thousand miles of Montana. However, regardless of the circumstances of the return, there is some kind of powerful emotional gravity that always pulls us homeward. I suppose it is some kind of evolutionary byproduct of the struggle to survive. Home is the security of family and tribe. Home is sustenance and health. Home is contentment. Whether we know it or not, we are hardwired to turn for home.

I suppose my sense of home was somewhat warped as a child and maybe this resulted in the extreme wanderlust that plagued me. Home for me as a kid was a fluid concept. As I mentioned earlier, I was mostly on my own as a child. My mother spent most of her time in a boozy haze, starring in her own movie in which she had all the speaking parts and I was only an extra. My father, on the other hand, was a workaholic musician who was not home enough. I spent most of my childhood playing with dolls and later sewing clothes for them. My love of solitude was probably developed out of necessity, rather than bequeathed to me as a strand of DNA.

There was, however, a brief time when I felt the warmth that is associated with home. Because my daddy was in education, summers were long and mostly happy. My parents were campers and owned a small travel trailer which Daddy towed with his LTD station wagon, complete with simulated wood grain panels. We would spend winter breaks at the beach and summers in the Smokies.

Then one summer, my parents bought a small piece of land on the banks of the Hiwassee River on which we would camp like gypsies for weeks on end. We would spend lazy days floating down the frigid, dam-controlled river in rafts and tractor inner tubes, which the locals thought was almost criminally stupid. Today, rafting the Hiwassee is a popular tourist attraction.

As I got older, I ventured farther into the woods surrounding the property. Daddy taught me how to tell the difference between poisonous and non-poisonous snakes. He also taught me how to pick up the Granddaddy Longlegs spiders and how to catch fireflies and June bugs. The forest became as comfortable to me as my own bedroom.

One summer, Daddy decided to build a cabin on the land. In addition to being an accomplished musician, he was an exceptionally good carpenter. When the river was low, Daddy and I would scavenge the riverbed for rocks which would be used for the foundation and fireplace. Over several summers, the house took shape and looked like it was finished on the outside. The inside, however, was only roughed-in. Wall boards didn't yet cover studs, wiring, and plumbing lines. Privacy for the toilet was provided by blankets which were nailed to the studs.

Despite the unfinished state of the house, my life felt complete. I had the constant companionship of my dog Jack, and I had the attention of my Daddy. Given the inattentiveness of

Mama, his gift of time and love meant everything to me. I also received a gift that wouldn't become apparent until many decades later when I decided to race a bike across the wilderness way out west. I learned how to be confident when alone in the woods. In many ways, the woods felt more like home than anywhere else.

I made it across the border and into the town of Eureka, Montana where I spent the night in a motel. The first order of business was to buy myself a celebration beer at the only convenience store in town. When I got settled in to the room, I turned on my phone and it blew up with texts. Friends all over the country had been following my GPS tracker and saw that I had made it across the border. I read each one and drew strength from each one. I drank a toast.

Cheers to my friends, cheers to America, cheers to the bears for not showing up, and cheers to me.

I was six days and 250 miles in, only about 2,500 more to go.

Jesus, that's a long way to go.

CHAPTER 9

The ninety-one-mile ride from Eureka to Whitefish, Montana would be no different from the other days so far on the divide—populated with Grizzlies. The stress of worrying about the Grizzly bears, the constant alertness, was beginning to wear on me. There were constant reminders of different animals present in the form of turds. In my preparation for the TD, I taught myself what each animal's scat looked like. Now, in the real world where such arcane knowledge would come in handy, I found that I had forgotten most of it. For certain, I recognized the bear, moose and elk scat, but none of the other. This was such an enchanted area of the trail, yet eerie at the same time. The forest became dense with Western red cedars, ferns and alders. In the middle of this thick forest was a clear, cold, swift creek running along the side of the deteriorating gravel road. I could feel the eyes of hidden creatures watching me as I rolled by.

My voice was still not back to normal and uttering a word was a challenge. Being bear aware meant having to be noisy at all times. I continued my butchery of Mother Goose. Sadly, I could only remember the first line of so many. *Pro tip: if you plan on racing the TD, a good working knowledge of mother goose rhymes is a must. Otherwise your recitation might devolve into banal lines about being eaten by bears.

Hush a bye Gracie on mountaintop
When the bear growls the mountain will rock
When the Grizz lunges Gracie will fall
Into bear's stomach helmet and all

I also attempted singing old camp songs which lead me to remember an old childhood friend. I began to speak my thoughts out loud. It startled me when I said her name.

"Sue Mills." I don't know why it struck me so. I repeated her name.

"Sue Mills."

It was as if speaking the name released a magic spell, unlocking a treasure box of days past. I began to sift through the memories we shared as young girls as if they were a stack of yellowed photographs. Girl Scout camp, trips to the river, first bras, boyfriends, and the time we hid in the back of a Pinto station wagon when we knew my brother was going to drive it to go hang out with his friends. Unbelievably, we got away with it until Sue farted. Farts are generally the funniest thing in the world, but when one is released in a venue where it is inappropriate to laugh, it becomes an irresistible force, like a black hole sucking up all resolve to maintain feminine reserve.

"Ooh, that's a stinker," she whispered.

"Omigod, Sue! Why did you do that?" I whispered back.

"I couldn't help it, it just slippied out."

"Did you say 'slippied?'"

We laughed so hard we almost peed ourselves. My brother heard us and pulled over. He raised the hatch to see our red-faces and tear-stained cheeks. He was not amused and threatened to kill me on the spot. Mostly, I think he was embarrassed to be pranked by a little girl. Only the power of flatulence saved him from the greater mortification of being bested by his sister in front of his friends. It probably saved me from a thrashing as well.

As I was talking out loud and trying to avoid assorted scat, the road turned upward. Eureka had been the lowest point of the entire race at 2,500 ft. above sea level, so it was all uphill from there. As I climbed the weather began to change. The sky grew dark and threatening. Small hailstones fell on me. This frightened me more than bears. For all the words written to satisfy our morbid curiosity about bears, they are not the most likely thing to kill a person in the Rockies. Lightning is; and while it is possible to outsmart a bear, lightning is an indiscriminate, impersonal killer. The only defense against it is to not to be nearby when it gets wound up.

Thankfully, the hail quickly turned to rain. I continued to pedal on, and eventually the sky brightened and the rain subsided. The grade continued to steepen until I finally crested the Divide at a place called Whitefish Pass. It had been a long climb. The descent was well worth the climb, fast and satisfying, but I feared coming around a corner at high speed and separating a mama Grizzly and her cubs.

The bears were not on the road, but they were definitely in my head. The valley I was rocketing into is called Yakinikak Creek, which is so remote and wild, it is the place authorities relocate bears when the bears become a little too aggressive around people. This was not a comforting thought. Regular, law-abiding bears were bad enough, but now I was riding through bear prison. I decided that if I were to see a bear with a gang tattoo, I would ride off the nearest cliff and be done with it.

The road mellowed out in the valley for a bit before it began to ascend once again. It continued along with unbelievable views and scenery in all directions. At one point I could even see the gloomy peaks of Glacier National Park in the distance. The time and miles flew by. Two curious marmots jogged alongside me for a while.

"Hello, John. Hello, Mikey," I said to them.

A park ranger cruising the area stopped to chat and inform me of the recently oiled road ahead. He warned me the roads could be slippery.

In one sense it was great the roads would be oiled. This would eliminate the large amount of dust I had been breathing, yet on the other hand, the fresh oil could be a mess to ride a bike through. It was. My front tire threw oil on my bike and legs, the back tire created a rooster tail that flung the oil up my back and into my hair. I rode through this for about a mile when I came up on the truck dispensing the fresh sprayed oil. The driver saw me in his rearview mirror. I made begging gestures I hoped he would interpret correctly. He did, and pulled his truck over to let me pass. Now the pressure was on to stay ahead of him. I was comfortably ahead on flat ground, but when the road became a hill, my lead was precarious. It was the world's most pathetic drag race, rocketing down the road at the blistering pace of 5 mph.

Finally, I reached Red Meadow lake and campground at an elevation of 5,600 ft. The spot looked so Hollywood perfect, it could've been the set for every summer camp movie ever made. The lake was crystal clear and looked so refreshing after my hot, oil-coated ascent. If it had been later in summer, I would have been tempted to take a dip, but because the air temperature was only fifty-or-so degrees, I decided to skip my 'Rose on the Titanic' impersonation. The empty campground was spooky, like a ghost town that was home to an ax murderer who preyed on unsuspecting explorers. I stopped to take a break, but my grim fantasies made me subconsciously hurry with creeping paranoia.

I left the campground and ascended into snow cover. This was my first snow crossing on the Divide and I was excited. That wouldn't last. The snow was patchy yet still required post-holing. The term alludes to exactly what you might imagine; a narrow, vertical, and deep insertion in of a pole (or leg) into the earth (or snow). This post-hole metaphor often plays out when a winter hiker steps on what she might first believe to be hard-packed snow, but sinks deep. Her leg creates a post-hole in the snow. And once realized, she is in for a fairly agonizing and exhausting hike until she finds firmer conditions. I did this while pushing my heavy rig at the same time. This miserable process continued for about a half mile until the road became completely passable again. I was utterly drained. I mounted my bike and tried to recover as I softly pedaled through the wintry silence. The feeling of solitude was so powerful, I was sure that I was the only person for tens of miles. My reverie was broken by the sound of a train in the distance. I laughed it off as some kind of auditory trick that the wind and the trees had conspired to play on me.

It's interesting how adaptable we are. I suppose it is humanity's greatest asset and the main reason why we became the planet's apex species despite a pathetic lack of strength, speed, or onboard weapons. I had only been in this environment, with its vast, silent wilderness and ramshackle towns for eight days, yet the rhythm had become as natural as breathing. Imagine my surprise when I rounded a bend and rode up on a mansion.

Rich people like the mountains just like us poor dirtbags, but they generally confine their 6,000 square-foot second homes to the vicinity of stylish towns with access to the finer things like ski resorts, haute cuisine and tasteful art galleries. This second home in the middle of nowhere could only mean one thing: I was coming into the ski town of Whitefish, Montana. As I rode on, I passed more mansions. The train I thought I had hallucinated was real after all; an Amtrak passenger train carrying summer tourists to and from this charming, slightly pretentious mountain town.

I strode into the swanky Firebrand Hotel and up to the desk. The hotel was immaculate in its tasteful western décor. Reclaimed barn wood panels graced the floor and walls. Horned cattle skulls adorned the walls. The couches and chairs were trimmed in distressed leather to give the place that urban sophistication-meets-rustic Montana panache.

I, on the other hand, was not as stylish as the average guest. I hadn't come in from a round of golf or a guided, air-conditioned Range Rover excursion in the mountains. I more closely resembled a homeless person who would probably get the bum's rush out of a swell place like this. I was filthy. The oil from the road made a Rorschach stripe up my back and matted my hair. Grime and dust and sweat permeated every cell of my body. Because I had lost my flip flops the first day, I had to wear my riding shoes into the lobby. I left a little trail of dried dirt clods on the reclaimed barn wood floor.

I wore my dirt as a badge of honor. Nobody was going to look down on me.

I just rode a bike ninety miles through the wilderness with two crossings of the Continental Divide, bitch. Alone. Top that, you snobs.

The fact that there were no snobs to direct these aggressive thoughts to was slightly disappointing, and then the irony struck me that I was engaging in a kind of snobbery that I imagined would be directed at me.

Eh, better go to bed.

CHAPTER 10

The next morning, I slept in until about 7 a.m. I made my way downstairs to eat a nice big breakfast. In fact, I ordered two meals. Waffles and a loaded omelet. Both of the entrees came with bacon. For most of my life I have been a slow eater and even though starved to replace the calories the TD was burning, my gustatory pace did not accelerate. I worked on these meals until I finally tapped out. It was getting late and I really needed to hit the road and put some miles under my belt. I asked the waitress if they had any tortilla wraps so I could just put all of my left overs in the wrap. This would make for a fabulous snack for later. The waitress brought me the wrap, aluminum foil and a ziploc bag. She had noticed I didn't eat all of the bacon and suggested I put the leftover bacon in another bag so it wouldn't get soggy. "Brilliant," I said and slipped the bacon into my jersey pocket.

By the time I rolled out of Whitefish it was mid-morning. It was an absolutely perfect day for riding. The temperature was around 55 degrees, and the sky was clear and many shades of blue. My plan for today's ride was to make it to Holland Lake Lodge about 110 miles down the trail. The first fifty miles would be on pavement making those miles quicker. I passed through the little towns of Columbia Falls, Swan Lake, and Ferndale. A road cyclist heading to Ferndale came up beside me. We rode together and chatted for about ten miles. It was nice having company.

I rode past several farms that teemed with life. It seemed like all of the animals had just given birth to babies. It was so much fun watching these animals with their young. One farm had pigs. As I stopped to photograph a group of little pink perfect piglets, they ran up to me. They were all lined up along the fence begging for food. I apologized to them that I could not spare any of my calories with their adorable faces. Looking back at how I unnecessarily hoarded food in the Ludicrous Food Bag, I probably could have shared a pound or two. Once they figured out that I was not going to be a food source, the piglets lost interest and drifted away. Except two. They stood there together, content to look into my eyes.

"Hello, John. Hello, Mikey," I said.

In my research for the Divide I was told that animals (wild, not domesticated like my little piggy buddies) will most likely be seen at dawn and dusk. Dusk falls much later in the north than what I'm used to at my more southerly latitude. When the TD started, sunrise was around 5:30 a.m. and sunset at 10:00 p.m. As I rode along, I noticed it was getting a bit darker. I looked at the time and was surprised to see it was 8 p.m.

Crap. I am only at 90 miles. I better pick it up and quit daydreaming.

I pedaled with purpose. The forest became progressively darker. My computer indicated that I needed to turn left off of the relatively bright road, onto an overgrown singletrack trail. The trail was a tangle of fallen trees, tall grass, and shrubs which required me to dismount my bike. The sounds of the forest drifted away and it became as silent as a tomb. It looked like a dangerous place and it was dark. Very dark.

It was dusk. Time for the wild animals to come out.

To say I was scared would be a gross understatement. Panicked was more appropriate. I was in full *fight or flight* mode, only you can't fight or flee from a Grizzly. I did the only thing I could. I yelled at the top of my lungs. I couldn't recall any stupid nursery rhymes so I spat out random pleading words to God, or the bears, which at this point seemed interchangeable in their ability to destroy or deliver me.

"Yo Bear!"
"Oh God, No Bear!"
"Oh God, No!"

"OH GOD!"

Each step I took felt like it would be my last. Then I remembered what Scott Thigpen had told me about bears just before I departed for the Tour. "You'll be fine unless you are wrapped in bacon."

Haha! I'm going to be fine.

Wait a minute.

I had completely forgotten about the bacon in my jersey pocket until now.

I *was* wrapped in bacon.

Fuck.

I jerked the smelly package out of my pocket and threw it as far as I could. I yelled like a banshee as I ran with my bike through the shadowy forest. I have never been so scared in my life. Not even close. If any bears were in earshot, they surely were terrified by the unholy screech that pierced the air like a siren.

I made it out of the black trail back onto the gravel road. By this time, it was almost completely dark. The bears hadn't gotten me, but I wasn't safe yet. A different kind of animal—one that I hadn't given much thought—began to attack mercilessly. Mosquitoes were now feasting on every part of my body. These otherworldly parasites drilled through my clothes, even the thick padding on the seat of my bike shorts. Seriously, I even had bites on my feet through my shoes. I put on my rain gear for a little added protection, hopped on my bike and took off down the road.

But there was no outrunning this predator. The swarm was omnipresent. The faster I rode, the more violent the hundreds of tiny collisions became. The bugs slamming into my rain jacket as I plowed through made a sound like rain hitting the earth. Earlier, when the light was dwindling, I had removed my sunglasses. Now this flying horde forced me to stop and put them back on to keep the bugs out of my eyes.

I honestly didn't feel like I had the time to dig in my bag for my clear lenses, lest the mosquitoes carry me off like the flying monkeys that abducted Dorothy in *The Wizard of Oz*. So, I rode in the dark with my sunglasses, like Arnold in *The Terminator*, except I had no desire to threaten these dudes with an "I'll be back." I never wanted to see them again. Flying down the road I could see the cloud of bugs as far as my light would carry. The only good news in this crazy hellish hour was no large animals were seen, though I almost would have rather endured an encounter with a Grizzly than this ridiculous gauntlet.

Eventually, my computer read 110 miles. I saw a campground, but Holland Lake Lodge was nowhere to be seen. I would have to ride another five miles to reach the lodge. I finally arrived at the lodge and went to the bar, which was packed with drunken revelers. While I waited, I observed they were all men and they didn't exactly fit the stereotype of the jeans-and-flannel-clad Montana male. Something about them was too stylish, too coiffed, too put-together. And the music. It wasn't some bro country anthem about beer or fishing. It was...dancy.

Then it hit me. I had walked in on a gay party.

O.K. Gracie, act casual. Don't let on that this is the first gay party you have ever crashed.

The host walked out, hand on hip, and asked, "Can I help you?" There wasn't much hospitality in his tone, which sounded more like, "What do you want?" What I really wanted was for him to tell me everything was going to be alright and give me a hug, but I would settle for a room.

"I would like to acquire a room for the night," I said.

What? Did I just use the word 'acquire'?

No one talks like that. Maybe I was finally off my rocker, hallucinating that I was a character on *Downton Abbey*, if there was an episode where they ride bikes in Montana and ask for rooms in their proper British accents. Whatever. I was too tired to be embarrassed. Hopefully he could tell by my appearance and weird vocabulary that I was worn ragged, traumatized, and needed someone to take pity on me.

"I'm sorry, we are completely booked for the weekend."

Piss.

So much for pity. While I was talking to this emotional rock of a man, the wind picked up. A storm was expected to move in overnight. I was running out of time. I dropped my head in dejection and frustration.

For a last-ditch effort, I smiled weakly and said, "Please tell me you are joking!" This seemed to melt him, if only a little. He apologized and suggested I go to the campground down the road then added as a conciliatory gesture, "Please come back in the morning for breakfast." I turned and exited the party as Lady Gaga blasted from the speakers. I mounted the bike and began the five-mile backtrack to the campground.

As I was heading to the campground a tiny fox jumped in front of me. Silhouetted against the blackness with only my bike light to illuminate him, he zigzagged back and forth across the light beam while periodically turning to look at me. He was playing with me! In my heart, I convinced myself this little fox was the spirit of my sweet little trail dog, Tsali, who used to run with me just like this back in the Appalachians. For a few precious moments, I forgot about how bone tired I was.

I arrived at the crowded, yet quiet, campground. All I wanted to do was set up my tent as quickly as possible before the rain set in. The wind was blowing with more purpose now, the rain wouldn't be far behind. But fate had two more tests scheduled for me before she would let me sleep.

In every campground, there is always somebody up and about, that one insomniac who roams the campground like a ghost in the wee hours. Sure enough, as I rode into camp I saw my solitary night owl, piddling with his gear. I rode up to him and asked him if I could acquire some space in one of the bear boxes. (Actually, I did not use the word acquire again. If anyone reading this hears me utter the word 'acquire,' you have permission to kick my pompous ass.)

Bear boxes are metal, stationary containers with intricate latches that even genius bears can't access. Being able to throw my food in a bear box instead of having to hang my bear bag would save me a lot of time.

"Nope, there aren't bear boxes in this campground."

Well great, now I'm going to be throwing rocks and risking head injury again.

"You could just leave your food in your vehicle."

Wow. It was clear that this was not the annual campout for the local chapter of MENSA. I wanted to strangle this dunce, but instead I pointed at my bike, hoping that he would eventually grasp the obvious.

"Oh, right, you're straddling your vehicle now."

Yes, Einstein.

I summoned my remaining poise and southern charm for one last try. "Could I store my food in your vehicle?" I smiled, hoping there were no mosquitoes in my teeth.

The dude reluctantly said yes. I threw the Ludicrous Food Bag at him before he could change his mind and ran off to set up my tent.

By this time, the wind was howling and it began to sprinkle. As I unpacked my tent, I was reminded of Dawson's assignment to set up a tent in the rain. I had bailed on that assignment and now would pay for my laziness. I engaged in an activity that could be described as either history's most moronic wrestling match, or the world's most awkward dance number, as the tent turned into a parachute. By the time I subdued and erected the tent and crawled inside, I had spent thirty minutes, and unintentionally migrated about 50 yards from where I started. My bike and other possessions were halfway across the campground. I didn't care. I had to sleep.

I looked at my watch as my eyes closed. It was 1:30 a.m.

Chapter 11

They say you can judge your age by what wakes you up in the morning. In childhood, you are awakened by your mother. In early adulthood, it's a baby. When you're middle aged, a job and its attendant, the alarm clock, wakes you up. And as you become a senior, it's your bladder. I was awakened on this morning by a screaming bladder. It was almost 9:00 a.m. and I had to pee like a Russian racehorse. I took this as a good sign that I was not dehydrated.

I rolled out of the tent into a steady rain in search of the bathroom. There was a large group of campers huddled under a pop-up shelter nearby. In the middle of the scrum was my night owl friend, pointing me out to the others. He had obviously shared the story of my strange arrival and the tent-wrestling show that I put on for him. He called me over to have breakfast. The others enthusiastically echoed his invitation.

"Give me a second, I gotta go pee."

They laughed. I'm not sure if they were laughing at my candor or my southern accent. After finishing my nature call, I joined them. They were a group of Young Life students and leaders on a camping trip. Young Life is a Christian organization that serves adolescents. It has an outdoors theme and runs several camps across the country.

The cook served me a hot plate of eggs and bacon. Despite having a minor episode of PTSD from my bacon incident the night before, I dug into the delicious breakfast. While I ate, I had an opportunity to tell them of my adventure so far and my plans to ride to the Mexican border. It's hard to impress teenagers, but judging from the gasps and the cries of "Whoa, dude!" I think I got their attention. I then told them I had MS. This blew their doors off. The questions started flying.

"How do you do this with MS?"
"How do you do this at all?"
"Don't you get scared?"
"Don't you get lonely?"

One of the most frustrating things for me about living with MS is the effect it has on me cognitively. I can think perfectly lucid and well-developed thoughts, but something happens to them between origination and vocalization. The result is that I get tongue-tied quite easily. Over the years, I have developed a shorthand to help me express the answers to the questions that others have asked me. More importantly, it has helped me answer the questions that I have asked myself when my depression and MS team up against me. This shorthand has been distilled into what sounds like simple slogans that aren't even original, but expresses a deep commitment to not just live with this disease, but thrive with it. When times get tough, I repeat them like mantras. My mantras are:

> *You Gotta Wanna* (desire)
> *Eyes on the Prize* (dedication)
> *Find a way* (overcome obstacles)
> *Leave MS in the Dust* (execution)

As I spoke with these kids, I shared my mantras with them and my mission statement, which is, *I ride for those who can't, and for those who think they can't.*

I don't know all the mysterious sources of the grit and determination that help me to fight the ravages of MS, but the activation of my willpower came on the day I got my diagnosis, and it came from a most unlikely source.

By the time I entered college, my mother and I had become estranged. Her bizarre behavior had just become too much to tolerate, especially considering I was at that confused age where I was trying to find my place in life. Despite Mama's weirdness, our family had connections to the upstanding families of town, and I was on track to be married into one of those families and live the perfectly scripted life of an upper middle-class southern lady. A chain-smoking eccentric with a drinking problem was not part of the script, so I marginalized Mama. I even started to refer to her by her first name, Rosemary, rather than Mama to put a little more distance between us.

In the spring of 1980, I was admitted to the hospital for vision issues. This was the second time I had been to the hospital, the first being many years earlier when I was a little girl. I was not diagnosed with any disease the first time. My vision got better and I went about my life. This time, however, diagnostics were more sophisticated. I received a spinal tap, which was the most painful thing I have ever experienced. I was given a prescription for steroids and discharged. I asked Rosemary what the steroids were for. She replied, "That's what they give people when they don't know what's wrong with them."

I figured the steroids must have worked. My vision returned to normal and I forgot about the whole thing. Then about a week later, I got a strange invitation from Rosemary. She wanted me and my boyfriend to come over for dinner. I didn't really want to hang out with her, but a home cooked meal is always welcomed by a poor college student. Although skeptical of her motives (because with her, who knew?), I paused my self-righteous banishment, grabbed my boyfriend, and went over.

After dinner, Rosemary invited us to go into the parlor to chat a bit. Odd. I didn't even know we had a parlor. She was acting even more screwy than usual. Once we settled on the couch, she stood up, pulled out a stack of brochures and threw them on the coffee table with a flourish. They all were printed with the words "Multiple Sclerosis" in bold letters. She didn't mince words.

"Gracie, you have been diagnosed with Multiple Sclerosis. I want you to read these from front to back, cover to cover, and look at each photo..."

A cold shudder rose up my spine and a heaviness—the dread of death—settled on my chest, making it difficult to breathe.

"...and then I want you to throw them away. You have been given this diagnosis, but it will not define you. I want you to live your life to the fullest, and you will figure it out along the way."

A baseball bat to the skull may have been subtler. Somehow, despite the shock, her simple speech burrowed its way into my memory and became written on my soul. Mama would've never guessed the effect these words would have on me. Likewise, when I heard these words in 1980, I never would've guessed that "along the way" would include a solitary 2,700-mile bike race in the Rocky Mountain wilderness. Words are funny things. We never know what impact they will have on another person. Sometimes, when spoken with clarity and conviction, they can be a blessing that lasts an entire lifetime. Without those words of assurance and confidence spoken by my mother, I doubt I would've done this or anything other than define myself as someone with MS.

Maybe Rosemary wasn't so crazy after all. Maybe she gave me the greatest gift I could ever receive. Maybe she was my original Trail Angel.

I finished my impromptu presentation to the Young Lifers by telling them of my work as an ambassador for a drug company that produces one of the disease-modifying therapies for MS. I traveled the country speaking at patient programs. I noticed that at each event, the audience members represented the full spectrum of MS, from the wheelchair-bound to the slightly affected. Some were truly debilitated, while others simply used MS as an excuse to stagnate. Very few understood that being your own advocate is the key to living your fullest life with MS. It was through these interactions I realized I had a unique story; one that might be inspirational to those who are being beaten up by the disease and those who are beating themselves up over the disease. I had always thought I was just doing what

Rosemary told me to do those many years ago, but as it turned out, I was doing something extraordinary.

The Young Lifers gathered around me as I was getting up to leave. They wanted to pray for me.

Yikes.

I have never been a religious person, so this was nearly as frightening as last night's horrors on the black trail. I really just wanted to get out of there and get on my bike, but that would've been the height of ingratitude, so I stuck it out. We gathered in a circle and held hands. I offered my own silent prayer.

Please Lord, let this be quick.

The leader prayed earnest words of gratitude and comfort and petitioned the Almighty for his providence over my journey. The shared words of encouragement, the warmth of human hands held in solidarity, and the palpable goodness of these people resonated through my soul and lifted me up towards a heaven that I scarcely believed existed. I began to cry, because what else would you do when overwhelmed by such love? The leader finished his prayer and the group chanted "Amen" in unison. I said "Amen" too. I was then mobbed by hugs, which led to a fresh round of tears.

I've met my share of phony baloney Christians in my life. These folks were the real deal; welcoming, generous, and uplifting.

I packed my bike and rode out of camp. I was followed by cheers and shouts of good luck as the group watched me go. I felt boundless gratitude for the encounter, and marveled at the chain of events—awful, exhausting events—that had made this sublime moment possible. I suppose that is a metaphor for life in general. We have to go through a lot of crap to get to the good stuff.

CHAPTER 12

It would be a fitting end to a Hollywood movie if my encounter with the Christians had been a turning point that transformed me into a trail-slaying TD goddess who stiff-armed Grizzlies and came from behind to finish in first place.

Yeah, but this wasn't Hollywood. This was real life, and the struggle in real life never ends. And so it was with me. I rode back to the lodge that turned me away the night before and sat down in the dining room. I ordered lunch and two sandwiches to go. Then I spent the next three hours doing what every serious competitor does in the middle of a 2,700-mile race. I surfed the internet.

I checked messages. Some of my friends wanted to know if I had become bear poop yet. I responded, "Nope, but the race isn't over yet."

I also called Coach Kym and recounted the events of the previous day. The Mileage. The Black Trail. The Bacon. The Bugs. The Wind. The Lodging Rejection. The Epic Tent Wrestling. As I spoke, the fear and frustration welled up inside me and I began to cry again.

Kym listened to my blubbering foolishness patiently. Kym is one of these superhuman oddities whose drive, intelligence, and energy propels them to greatness. She has an M.S. in sports psychology and a PhD in kinesiology with an emphasis on the mental health outcomes of MS patients who exercise, so she was tailor-made for me. She has been a business owner, teacher, coach, and even a professional cyclist. She has been my coach for ten years and has an almost intuitive ability to connect with me.

After I had cried myself out, Kym had me list the accomplishments I had completed. Three hundred and fifty miles ridden almost utterly alone in an unforgiving wilderness full of the scariest creatures in the entire western hemisphere. One hundred and fourteen miles ridden yesterday alone. And all of this while carrying my entire life support systems with me, and while being seriously handicapped by a nasty infection that was *still* lingering. Oh yeah, and MS.

We laughed about the bacon. "Gracie, you're doing great. Be proud of what you have done. You don't have to worry about whether you can do this or not. You are already doing it."

"I can. I will. I am," I replied.

Hey, that sounds good. I need to remember that.

It was nice to hang out in the lodge for a while. It was raining steadily outside and I really didn't feel like riding. This was a race, however, and races aren't usually won or even finished by being sedentary. I made a call to the motel in the next town, Seeley Lake, for a reservation. I acquired (there I go again) their last room. Thankfully, Seeley Lake was only thirty-or-so miles away, so it would be a light day. Even so, it was nearly 3 p.m. when I headed out, and today's ride would take me over the infamous Richmond Peak. I needed to get moving.

On my way out of the restaurant, I met two TD riders coming in. Their names were Duane and Zak. Words began pouring out of my mouth about my previous day's ordeal and I began to cry. AGAIN. Duane and Zak listened to my story and encouraged me.

"Grace, you've done all this by yourself?"

"Yes."

"You are awesome!"

"I don't feel awesome right now."

"You are killing this race!"

As we talked, I began to feel a little better. My confidence was building. Then I made a mistake. I told them that I was going to cross Richmond Peak. They looked at their watch.

"You're going over Richmond at this time of day? Alone?" They exchanged a raised eyebrows glance at each other that said "this chick is nuts."

The guys could sense that they had said too much. Maybe because I started crying again. They started to backtrack.

"Well, you're only going to Seeley Lake. You will be fine."

I don't think they meant it. We said our good-lucks and goodbyes. They walked into the restaurant and I rode off into the dreary rain toward Richmond Peak and whatever fresh hell awaited me there. I cursed myself for my stupid lack of pre-ride planning. I should have been looking at maps instead of Facebook. I was just winging it each day. Would this be the day I would get myself in trouble for it?

Rain has a way of quieting the forest and the human soul as well, turning it inward. As I absentmindedly rode along, I replayed the encounter with Duane and Zak. When they gave each other the knowing look that they were talking to a crazy person, it sparked a memory. I had seen that look before when I observed people talking about Rosemary. Now people were doing it to me. Was I crazy like my mother? Was I a fool for thinking I could complete this ridiculous challenge?

Then I remembered my mantra from my earlier conversation with Kym.

I can. I will. I am.

Amazing what a simple phrase can do when paired with belief. As I repeated the words, they took on the power of a magic spell, lifting my mood. I began to relish the day. It was in the 50s, raining, and I was climbing up four miles of the very difficult, washed-out, rock-strewn, treefall-littered slopes of Richmond Peak, but I was happy. In fact, the harder it got, the happier I became. Maybe I was as cuckoo as my mother, but at least I had found a healthier way to burn off the crazy than her cigarettes and alcohol.

I also noted the extreme mood swings that I had gone through during the day; from despair to joy to despair again and back to elation. This was dangerous. If anything would knock me out of the TD, it wouldn't be the bears, it would be poor emotional control. I made a mental note to be aware of the extremes and to try and keep it in the middle, or, as we say in the South, *between the ditches.*

Between the ditches, bitches. I can. I will. I am.

As I climbed toward the top of Richmond Peak, the temperature dropped. The rain turned to sleet. The view from the top of the climb was shrouded in clouds that rolled across the peak like great gray boulders. Upon reaching the top, I had to search for a singletrack side trail that was the official TD route. There were many ways to get to each day's destination, but only one official way. To take an off-route trail or road meant disqualification from the race. I promised myself that I would not succumb to the temptation to take the easy way. Additionally, I was diligent about following the map that had been loaded into my computer so I didn't miss a turn and unwittingly disqualify myself.

I found my trail and headed down the mountain. The trail was a challenging mix of fallen trees, steep terrain, and deep snow. There were bicycle tire tracks through the snow, which confirmed I was on the right trail. Several times, I had to dismount and post-hole my way through long snowy patches. As the elevation decreased and the snow became thinner, I felt cocky enough to try to ride one of the snow fields. Fishtailing out of control, I was flung off the bike like a mechanical bull rider. As I lay there on my back, laughing at my comeuppance, I made a snow angel. I stood up to look at it and felt warmth in my heart. I was where I was supposed to be. It was right. It was good.

I had become my own trail angel, gifting myself with the permission to make mistakes, to laugh at my errors while learning from them, and to be happy.

I came to the end of the snowy trail as it terminated into a fire road. The TD route went left. The town of Seeley Lake and my bed for the night was to the right, several hundred feet below me in the valley. I would pay for my comfort tonight with a long climb back to this spot tomorrow to rejoin the official route. I didn't care; I wanted a shower and a dry bed. I coasted down the mountain and into town.

When I rolled into the parking lot of the motel, I saw two bikepackers out front eating ice cream cones. They looked familiar. I thought they might be TD racers, so I rode over to them. It was Duane and Zak!

"How the hell did you get here?"

"We rode our bikes," came the coy reply.

"No shit. You left after I did and you didn't pass me." They smirked like two little boys caught with their hands in the cookie jar. Duane spoke.

"We didn't feel like camping and we didn't feel like fighting Richmond."

"We didn't want to deal with the snow or the singletrack either," Zak added. They had taken the highway to Seeley Lake, beating me by about 45 minutes.

"Frickin' cheaters!" I shouted at them, laughing. We all knew that their shortcut meant disqualification. They didn't care. We shared our stories of the day. They were glad that my mood had improved from the time they last saw me at Holland Lake Lodge. We discussed riding together the next day and I headed off to do my chores, which consisted of resupplying, eating, cleaning my bike chain, showering, and washing my riding clothes. Then I collapsed into a hard, dreamless sleep.

CHAPTER 13

When I awakened the next morning, it was Day 10. I realized that I was doing this thing. I was a legitimate TD racer! I had faced and overcome many of my fears (bears, getting lost, being alone, etc.) and I was slowly developing a rhythm. The infection was on its last legs and old foe MS hadn't reared its ugly head.

My plan for the day was to ride seventy miles and climb 4,000 ft. to the town of Lincoln, Montana. I looked forward to riding with Duane and Zak. I might be an introvert by nature, but even introverts have need for regular human contact. The long days in the wilderness were sometimes boring.

That didn't work out so well. Duane and Zak were exhausted and not ready to ride when I was, so we said our farewells and I pedaled off, alone again. The two friends dropped out of the Tour Divide not long after that. I was still in last place.

It was a rainy and cold morning, which was becoming my favorite riding weather. Cool temps were easier on the body and better for minimizing MS symptoms. MS is a process of inflammation. Like treating a sports injury with ice, cooling the body minimizes the ravages of inflammation on the nervous system. Theoretically. This advantage is probably negated if you are pushing your body over its limit for days on end.

As I rolled out of town toward the day's midpoint goal, the little town of Ovando, I noticed my vision was blurry. I figured my contacts were dirty and decided to wait until I got to town to clean them.

The ride to Ovando was pleasant and surprisingly easy. All gravel and paved roads, through the Clearwater River Valley and into the Blackfoot River watershed, where the valley opened up dramatically to reveal the large flat floodplain. After days of being bracketed by big mountains, wide open spaces were refreshing.

The sign welcoming visitors to Ovando read *Population: about 50; Dogs: over 100*. Dogs are every road cyclist's nightmare, often darting out from yards like furry bullets to plow into riders, sometimes causing serious injury for the rider and the dog. After worrying so much about being knocked off my bike by a Grizzly, wouldn't it be ironic to be taken out by a dog!

I headed for the town's only diner, the Stray Bullet Café. The first thing I did after getting seated was go to the bathroom to clean the annoying contacts. When I returned, a cheerful-looking woman with red cheeks and flowing white hair was sitting at my table, smiling at me.

"Hi Grace, I'm Kathy."

"Um, how do you know my name?"

She laughed and told me she had been watching my dot get closer to Ovando for several days. Every TD racer has to carry a GPS transmitter. This data is displayed on the race website. The interested (and monumentally bored) can track each racer's position via their dot on the website's map.

Kathy is the co-owner of Blackfoot Angler, the fly-fishing shop in town, and a dedicated "dot-watcher." She makes it a point to greet each TD racer as they come through town. Even in the fly-fishing mecca of Ovando (the nearby Blackfoot River was made famous in the novel and movie *A River Runs Through It*), life moves at such a sedate pace as to allow this lady time to run a business and function as a one-woman welcoming committee. It was completely charming, as was Kathy.

Kathy was also the TD gossip, filling me in on all the news of other racers. She told me that Mark Bates' dot was all over the place, yet he kept finding his way back to the route and was still racing. After filling my belly and chatting with Kathy, I mounted up and rode out of town.

My contact lens maintenance had been ineffective and my vision continued to be blurry. "Damn contacts," I muttered.

Then, while walking my bike up a steep climb, my right leg buckled.

Hello, Elvis.

Elvis Leg, that is. My "Elvis Leg" is one of my symptoms of MS. So is blurry vision. When my leg gave out, I realized my vision issues weren't the result of dirty contacts, but from the old friend. MS had come to pay a visit.

The first time I remember MS coming to call, I was a little girl, about ten years old. I was outside, playing with my dolls and my vision became blurry. I ran to Mama to tell her. True to form, Mama brushed off my complaints and sent me back outside. She must have been concerned though, because the next day, she told me she was going to take me shopping.

Mama had never taken me shopping before. She said we were going to Vanderbilt Children's Hospital in Nashville to check out my vision and I needed a new pair of pajamas.

At Vanderbilt, I put my new pjs on and was sent around the ward to play with the other kids. One room contained a child in an oxygen tent, another had a bedridden boy with tubes sticking out of him, another had a sweet-looking girl with no hair. After a few of these encounters, I ran back to my room and told Mama that I didn't want to wear my new pajamas anymore. I didn't feel sick enough to be there and wanted to go home. Mostly I didn't want to lose my hair.

We left the hospital without a diagnosis. That wouldn't come for many years.

Throughout the years, Elvis Leg has been the most outwardly visible sign of my disease. I call it Elvis Leg because when an episode strikes, my right leg becomes wobbly and reminds me of a young Elvis Presley, who titillated and scandalized a nation with his gyrations. Unfortunately, unlike the King's, my jitterbugging leg isn't under my command, but makes appearances on its own schedule. It has been the source of many embarrassments, causing me to spill across the floor at the most inopportune moments. Thankfully, it has remained more of an irritation than a disability. I've just picked myself up and kept on trucking.

A few years back, I participated in a six-day stage race called the Brek Epic, in the mountains of Colorado. There was a lot of climbing in the race; much of it which must be pushed, or *hike-a-bike* as we call it. My Elvis Leg was really flaring up and the bike became a crutch as I would push a step, drag Elvis, and repeat. It was a long and tortuous process, but I finished the race. I didn't win, but I did receive a big cowboy belt buckle. The front of the buckle resembled the Colorado license plate with the words 'Brek Epic' emblazoned on it. The words "240 miles," "40k vert," and "Bad Motherfucker" were stamped inconspicuously on the back.

That's me.
MS, meet the Bad MF.
I brought the unusual climbing style to the TD as I Elvis-ed my way up Huckleberry Pass, dragging my leg, looking like an undead cyclist in a zombie movie. The view at the top was spectacular, at least what I could see of it through my foggy eyes. The ride down even more so. I rolled carefully into Lincoln and straight to the Wheel Inn Restaurant. The proprietors had set up some self-serve trail magic in the form of a tent with cookies, tools, and a bike wash. Inside, I wolfed down a big hamburger, then limped through a grocery store to resupply the Ludicrous Food Bag, and beelined it for bed. I set my alarm for 5:30 a.m., hoping to get a jump on the day for my big push into Helena.

Yeah, right. I seem to recall some famous line about the best laid plans of mice and men.

CHAPTER 14

In my optimistic plans for my ride on Day 11, I forgot to include MS into my calculations. MS reminded me that we still had unfinished business when the alarm went off at 5:30 am. My vision was blurry, Elvis was still being Elvis, and my entire body felt weak and depleted. I called Kym.

"Kym," I croaked when she answered.

"You sound like shit."

"MS decided to make an appearance on the Tour Divide."

"Go back to bed and take the day off."

I did. It was a rainy, dreary day anyway. Good day to sleep.

Chapter 15

Late in the afternoon of my rest day, my MS symptoms started to subside. Vision had improved and Elvis had left the building. Strength and energy returned. I ate another big hamburger at the Wheel Inn and went to bed at 8 p.m. Tomorrow: Helena.

I peeked outside when the alarm rang at 5:30 am. Still raining. The ride to Helena, Montana would be a big one; another seventy-miler with three Continental Divide (CD) crossings and some 7,000 ft. to climb. I packed, ate, and rode into the gloomy rain, which to me, wasn't gloomy at all. After twelve days almost all to myself, I had done some deep introspection. One of the things that surprised me was how much I liked being alone.

In my youth, I considered myself to be an extrovert. To be fair, the terms extrovert and introvert hadn't been popularized in the 1970s, yet there was a distinction between a girl who was outgoing and a girl who was just weird. The entire female social structure in the South revolved around making oneself an attractive choice as a mate. Women's lib was still a northeastern urban idea; the bucolic South was still enamored with a romantic, yet rigid set of norms which calcified into a de facto caste system which made it easier to distinguish the good folks from the trash. Cotillions, debutante balls, and other assorted puffery were the coins of the realm. Without these resume' builders under one's belt, there was no admittance to the club, and without being in the club, there was no admittance to the resume' builders. It was, by design, a closed system.

In order to be a player in this game and to move up in its invisible ranks, an outgoing personality was indispensable. Girls were coached to always have a pleasant disposition and be eager to join clubs that exhibited a lively mind and a perky spirit. A girl who was bookish or taciturn carried the kiss of death, as a reticent nature implied unsociability and thus unsuitability for marriage.

Our family should have been on the wrong side of the tracks, so to speak. If Rosemary had been married to anyone else, it would've been a no-brainer. But Daddy's position at the university gave our family a fig leaf of respectability, so we were, by the skin of our teeth, in the club.

Unwittingly, I did my part to maintain the family's tenuous grip on respectability. In high school, I reached the pinnacle of the pecking order and became a cheerleader, although I always carried a nagging feeling of not quite belonging. While the other girls lorded their reign at the top of the school hierarchy over the hoi polloi, I was planning my next escape to the forest that bracketed the Hiwassee, even as my hands altered the other cheerleaders' uniforms.

I allowed myself to be carried along by the cultural current into college. I attended the University of Alabama and joined that bastion of social conformity, the sorority. Life was a series of mindless parties. Conversations were lifeless repetitions of the same old gossip and banal aspirations. At the time, I didn't question the grinding monotony, but something didn't feel right in Happy Party Land. I couldn't put my finger on it at the time, but there was an unspoken resignation among my peers that life would be comfortable, but at a cost of regret and utter boredom that would compound like interest in a bank.

It was difficult for me to force myself into this uncomfortable role of the always smiling, always talkative, fun blonde, but I thought that was just how it was supposed to be. To get to the promised land of marriage and a life of suburban ease—to take one's place in the southern order of things—one had to put in the work of formals and teas and all that plastic b.s. It never occurred to me at that time, there might be other ways to live.

It would take many more years of discovery to find my authentic self and discover that I was indeed an introvert after all.

Here I was, a dropout from the sorority lifestyle, living a life that would make a stylish housewife cringe. I was poor, unemployed, temporarily homeless, living on a bicycle, riding through a cold drizzle, dodging potholes, slinging mud everywhere, and all alone in the Rocky Mountain wilderness. I was about as far from Alpha Sigma Snobba as I could have been.

I couldn't have been happier. To pass the time as I pedaled along, I tried to list all of the emotions I was feeling. I came up with content, brave, joyous, interested, serene, grateful, cheerful, confident, enthusiastic, euphoric, proud, amused, and awed. These mountains and this trail had healed my soul at the same time they were beating up my body.

I crossed the first of three CD passes almost unconsciously while I was lost in my thoughts. The landscape was dotted with pleasant-looking cattle ranches nestled among the dark green conifers of the Helena National Forest. Cattle guards, large metal grates sunk into the road bed, became more frequent. These allowed travelers to pass while keeping the cows within their boundaries. All along the way, cattle loitered in the road. They would stop chewing as I weaved among them, but could never be bothered to get out of the way. Dodging cows, and the smelly byproduct that they deposited everywhere like a brown minefield, substituted for the challenge of more technical trails.

The rain never let up. Although I kept my raingear on, I was still soaked to the bone. Wetness carried the risk of hypothermia, which was one of the most dangerous things I would face out here. The symptoms of hypothermia—clumsiness, low energy, weak pulse—are so dangerous because they come on slowly, and increasing mental confusion often prevents the victim from taking action. So, I kept a vigilant eye on my functioning for any signs of decreasing core temperature, but a nagging conundrum kept me second-guessing throughout the day; if my mental capacity diminished along with my body temperature, would I even be capable of noticing?

Temperature regulation was a constant dance of taking off and putting on layers. Climbing uphill created excess heat, which prompted me to take off a layer. Descending fast downhills created a wind chill, which made me put the layer back on. My go-to warm layer was a hooded microfiber jacket which I kept in my Sweet Roll for easy access. It was one of my favorite pieces of gear. I called it my puffy hoodie.

On the descent of the second CD pass, I took a nasty spill. A washed-out section of the road surprised me and threw me off the bike. Mountain bikers are used to laying down a bike, but the stakes were much higher out here. A wreck could hurt rider or bike, either of which could turn ugly for a person alone and miles from civilization, especially in a cold rain.

Luckily, I was uninjured, but the incident made me wonder if my slow reflexes might have been caused by the onset of hypothermia. I looked at the GPS. It had a feature called the "Oh shit, come get me" button in the event that a rider got in big trouble. I wasn't thinking about using it, but I wondered if I would be able to if I was truly hypothermic. The cost of using the "Oh shit, come get me" button was also prohibitive. At $25,000 per rescue, I would have to be halfway in the bear's stomach or hanging off a cliff by my fingernails to push it.

Thoughts of injurious crashes, hypothermia, and $25,000 buttons sobered me from my earlier euphoria. I decided to make a more focused push into Helena before something really bad *did* happen. At the top of Priest Pass, the day's third CD crossing, a heavier rain started to fall. I wanted to make a quick transition into my puffy hoodie, so I quickly unclipped and unrolled the side closure of the Sweet Roll. *Grab puffy hoodie, put on puffy hoodie, zip up, put rain jacket on, zip up, off we go.* I felt like a NASCAR pit crew.

Yeah, right. NASCAR pit crews don't leave off one of the four tires. I did something equivalent.

About halfway down the mountain, I realized I had forgotten to close the Sweet Roll. Once I noticed my error, I skidded to a stop to see if anything had flown out. I did a quick gear check. Everything seemed to be there. I closed the bag and rode on.

I pedaled into the outskirts of Montana's capital in a steady rain, looking for lodging. The smudgy green and red reflections of traffic signals in the wet streets seemed exotic after so many days of being immersed in natural light. It reminded me of an impressionist painting.

After a few pointless miles of foraging for a place to stay, I rolled up to a coffee shop. The benefits of continuing my search inside the shop included an escape from the rain, a chance to let Google do the work more efficiently for me, and a hot cup of joe would feel so good to these waterlogged old bones. As I was waiting on my coffee, an older couple approached and asked me if I was racing the TD. I asked them if my heels and pearls gave me away! We laughed and I affirmed that I was on the TD. They asked me to join them at their table. Their names were Sid and Beth.

Sid and Beth were lifelong Helena residents, retired and enjoying their golden years together. I mentioned that I was looking for lodging and they exchanged a glance. Beth spoke up and asked if I would like to stay at their house, which was right on the TD route.

Trail Magic strikes again! Every instance of Trail Magic is special and appreciated, but this was above and beyond. This was five-star magic. It got even better after I pedaled over to their house.

Beth gave me some cozy sweatpants to wear while my clothes were being washed. Earlier in the day, she had made beef stew and cornbread which she shared with me. I had a comfy room with a private bath.

This could be one of those scenarios where the sweet old couple are actually serial killers who lure people to their house to dismember them.

As I relaxed in my dry, toasty, borrowed sweatpants on the soft bed, I reached the conclusion that if they were to kill me in my sleep, this level of luxury would be worth it. I fell unconscious shortly thereafter.

I woke up the next morning, alive after all. I didn't hear the gruesome sound of a chainsaw being revved as Sid walked it ominously down the hall, or any other horror film cliché. I did hear the sounds of pots and pans being employed in the production of breakfast. The glorious smell of frying bacon permeated my nose and then penetrated my brain, lifting me from my deep slumber.

Beth had cooked a big breakfast with eggs, toast, and fruit to compliment the bacon. The three of us shared it and some quiet talk about the day ahead of me.

"Grace, how long until you reach Mexico?" Sid asked.

"I don't know. Three or four weeks, maybe." As I said those words, the enormity of the remaining task hit me hard.

Not hours, not days. Weeks.

Sid and Beth looked at me with that parental poker face which tries to conceal concern but betrays worry anyway. Beth straightened up and exhaled as if suppressing an unwanted emotion. The air was heavy with deja vu, as if a similar conversation had taken place years ago when their own child was leaving the nest to go to a place they could not reach.

I loaded up. As we said our goodbyes, I was once again moved to tears by the hospitality of total strangers who had become friends.

What is this quality that motivates such generosity? What is it that moves some people to give their time, their food, even their homes to the strangers who ride in and out of their lives like a spring breeze? Is it a vicarious curiosity? Pity? Respect? Boredom? Loneliness? Or are they just wired that way?

I've only dabbled in altruism; I haven't practiced it enough to comprehend its depths. But I do know most people live most of their lives based on the principles of reciprocity—you do for me, I do for you. How lovely and remarkable it is when one is the recipient of a true gift; one where no payment is expected, accepted, or even possible. It is such a beautiful expression of the best part of human nature, and so rare, it seems almost inhuman. The "Angel" in Trail Angel is a most appropriate name. Maybe they are really from heaven.

CHAPTER 16

Day 13 was scheduled to be another big push—70 miles and three more CD crossings with 7,100 ft. of climbing. The day's route started on a road called Grizzly Gulch. The plethora of Grizzly themed place names was wearing thin. Grizzly Road, Grizzly Drive, Grizzly Pass, Grizzly Basin, etc. Back home, if we named as many places after our most recognizable animals, there would be a lot of Raccoon Roads, Skunk Streets, and Possum Parkways. Not nearly as majestic.

The Grizzly identifiers had one benefit. They reminded me that I was still in Grizzly country. The truth was my bear awareness had been slipping. The bell on my bike was still ringing, but I had completely tuned out the sound of it. My brain had also tuned out the possibility of running up on a bear. The country had opened up, giving a much wider field of vision. It was, in a word, relaxing. In the close forests of Canada and northern Montana, my range of sight extended only a few feet, and most of that was only on the road ahead of me. I was always on edge because a Grizzly could be mere feet away from me and I would not know it. The anxiety was exhausting.

But you know how the universe is ordered, right? Things you worry about seldom occur. On the Black Trail, I was sure that a bear was in there with me and it sent me into a panic. Nothing happened there or over any of the hundreds of miles I had traveled. A friend of mine says, "Don't borrow trouble," but some of us always do, expending precious energy on possibilities rather than likelihoods.

Things only get interesting when we drop our guard. Shortly after I crossed my first CD pass of the day, I saw it.

A Grizzly Bear.

He was a big boy, 500 pounds of him. Healthy. Regal. The fur that stands up straight on the telltale ridge on a Grizzly's back glistened with raindrops. He was downslope, below the road on which I was riding, digging in a rotting log for bugs to eat. Here I was at last, face to face with the beast that the Shoshones respected and feared so much, the monster who had terrorized Lewis and Clark. My mind raced to retrieve all the tips for encountering a Grizzly.

Don't make eye contact.
Talk to it in a firm voice.
Back away slowly.
For God's sake, don't run!
Play dead if he attacks.

The "Gentleman," as Merriwether Lewis sarcastically called him, was about 100 yards from me. I remembered reading somewhere that a Grizzly can outrun a horse, so I figured he could get to me in less than five seconds if he wanted.

Thankfully, he didn't want to. When he looked up and saw me, he turned and ran down the hill into a thicket of trees. How ironic. In my heart, I had been running from a Grizzly since I left Banff. In reality, a Grizzly ran away from me.

Perplexed, I looked for several minutes at the place where he disappeared, expecting him to come back out. He did not. The terrifying meeting that I had replayed over and over in my brain was shattered by a cowardly bear. I shrugged and rode on, stealing an occasional glance over my shoulder to make sure he wasn't coming up from behind. As the adrenalin rush wore off, my body did one of those involuntary shivers that Appalachian old-timers call "a possum running over my grave." I had seen a Grizzly and lived to tell the tale! Honestly, it was a little anticlimactic, and I was o.k. with that.

I passed hundreds of cows, crossed dozens of cattle grates, and met a few ranchers along the way. These modern-day cowboys didn't ride horses. They drove the dusty roads in their beat-up pickup trucks, doing what ranchers do.

I saw one rancher off in the distance driving toward me. I saw the rising dust cloud in his wake for several minutes before I saw his truck. It looked like he was dragging something behind him. In the distance, I could only make out a black speck that weaved in and out of view. As he got closer, I realized it was a dog. "O.K.," I thought, "this guy is checking on his cattle and the dog has followed him."

As he drove past me, the dog veered off course and came straight at me. The sonofabitch bit me on the ankle. The driver saw what happened and stopped to curse the dog.

"Goddammit, Rocky, I told you to stop biting people," the man scolded. The rancher apologized and explained that he was running his dog. Rocky, in addition to being a slow learner, looked unrepentant. In fact, he looked like he would like to have another go at me.

"Running your dog?"

"Yeah, getting him some exercise."

"Is he training for a marathon?"

"Naw, I just want to keep him from getting too lazy and fat."

The irony seemed to be lost on the man who never got out of his truck; his own superfluous pounds were obvious in his jowly face and thick, sweaty arms. As I pedaled off, I wondered if I would ever stop encountering these odd people. I hoped not. I could do without any more dog bites, though.

As I closed in on Butte, the road became crowded with hikers and trail runners. Finally, I crested a hill that overlooked the whole town. Shafts of sunlight pierced the clouds and illuminated the valley. A smile crept across my face. I had survived a bear sighting and a dog attack and would live to ride another day. I started down the hill on a wave of euphoria which was short-lived as I promptly made a wrong turn that took me off course. It was demoralizing having to climb up a hill that I shouldn't have been on in the first place, but Trail Magic awaited me once I rejoined the route.

A handsome couple was out hiking their dogs and I struck up a conversation with them. I asked them how far it was to the Super 8 Motel. They responded that it was about eight miles on the other side of town. I must have made my disappointment too obvious. They chuckled and offered to take me to the motel in their truck.
"Yes, please."

CHAPTER 17

I made a dumb mistake getting into that truck, one that would have cost me sixteen extra miles and an unnecessary climb, if it weren't for the generosity of the motel's shuttle driver. The kindness of the hiking Trail Angels who brought me to the Super 8—and my own laziness—overwhelmed my better judgment to look ahead at the route, which ran right past the Super 8.

I should have just finished off those last eight miles myself.

Because I skipped them when I accepted the lift, I would've had to climb back up the hill to the point where I got into the truck with the hikers and then turn around and ride right back to the motel to continue the race. Luckily, the motel's shuttle driver wasn't busy that morning. He took me to the spot where I stopped, which happened to be on a steep incline, difficult to manage in a van which was not technically off-road capable.

I quickly gathered my stuff and bid him a hasty thank you, wanting to save him any more consternation, which I could sense was growing as he began to regret his decision to bring me out here. Then I rode back down the hill, through Butte and past the Super 8 on the outskirts of town. The shuttle driver was out front, smoking a cigarette. He snorted at me, gave me a big smile and a wave as I cruised on by.

My legs were tired. Two big mileage and big elevation days had taken their toll. Thankfully, today's ride would "only" be fifty-three miles with one CD crossing. The road out of Butte was heavy with car traffic, which unnerved me and burned my energy reserves at a rapid rate.

I was glad to leave the highway and re-enter the forest. Bears might stoke deep-seated, natural fears thousands of years in the making, but cars brought out an unnatural exhaustion from, and loathing for, so-called "modern" life. The wilderness equivalent would be if I were passed from behind by hundreds of humongous, fast-moving Grizzlies while wondering which one was going to attack me. The comparison may sound absurd, but it illustrates the absurd level of danger that cyclists have been conditioned to accept without question.

In our rush to increase our comfort and ease of living, we have allowed our dependence on these insensate metal hulks to dominate every facet of our lives, design our cities and towns, scratch lasting scars into the landscape, and kill our friends and family by the hundreds of thousands. I was aware of my own hypocrisy as well. Both last night and this morning, I was all too eager to jump into a vehicle to save my own energy and time. It has been a devil's bargain that we have all been only too willing to make. It is only when we live outside car culture for a while that we begin to count the costs. Thankfully, the cost for me on this day was only stress and a diminished mojo. The costs for all those who never live outside the comfort of their automotive bubble are much higher, and most don't even know it. The costs for those killed by cars are greater still.

The biggest challenge of this day, aside from running the internal combustion gauntlet outside Butte, was a notorious descent down Fleecer Ridge. All of the past TD finishers I talked to mentioned it. It even has a nickname among the bikepacking set—Thermarest Hill. Thermarest is a large manufacturer of lightweight air mattresses for camping. Apparently, Fleecer is infamous for destroying mattresses. I'm not sure how, but the rumors were enough to get my attention.

The descent lived up to its billing; a nasty mile covered in loose scree, with a gradient that reached 38% in places. Riding a hill that steep would be suicidal. Walking it was one notch below falling off a cliff. I got off the bike and walked. Having gravel-sized scree underfoot turned it into a virtual ski slope without any of the charm associated with a ski slope. I was glad to reach the bottom without mishap.

Having successfully navigated Fleecer, the ride to the Wise River Club/Bar/Café/Motel (one stop shopping at its finest!) was uneventful, probably my least difficult day of the Tour so far. It was nice to have a simple day, because I was tired. Really tired.

Oh, and I didn't ruin my air mattress either, but not because of my expert descent of Thermarest Hill. It's hard to destroy something you no longer have.

But I wouldn't figure that out until I needed it.

Chapter 18

Day 15 dawned sunny. For the past three days, I had been riding in various stages of rain, from drizzle to downpour. The sunlight was welcome, but did nothing to alleviate the physical exhaustion that resided in every cell in my body. I had never done any kind of athletic endeavor of this scope—not even close—and its inexorable toll was accumulating. I was more than 800 miles in and my tank was bone dry.

800 miles.
1,900 to go.
How am I ever going to do this?

I was reminded of a riddle I had heard long ago. "How do you eat an elephant? One bite at a time." I added that to my list of mantras.

One bite at a time
You gotta wanna
Eyes on the prize
Find a way
Leaving MS in the dust
I ride for those who can't and those who think they can't
I can. I will. I am.

My little pep talk didn't cure me, but it got me out of bed and on the bike. Much of this day's route would be traveled along paved roads, which would be a mental, as well as physical, break from the pounding of the trail. Once on the bike, I put my head down and stared three feet in front of my spinning tire for hours as the monotonous miles slipped by.

I didn't have a plan. I had been too tired to look at maps the night before. I was just winging it again. I kept pushing south, hoping to find a soft landing spot somewhere down the way. Each campground I passed beckoned like a siren. I was so tired. I needed sleep, but I just kept turning the pedals in a mindless, hazy shuffle.

This is a race?

This wasn't a race, it was an exercise in finding one's limits. Although I felt no desire to quit, I could feel the cold footsteps of exhaustion creeping closer.

I have heard of athletes suffering hallucinations during very long races. Extreme fatigue can push a brain (not always the best functioning organ in the best of conditions) past its limits. The line between sleep and wakefulness becomes blurred and the brain malfunctions, retrieving broken fragments of memory and imagination and inserting them into current reality.

As I entered the village of Polaris, Montana, I had the foggy notion it might be the home of the large manufacturer of ATVs and snowmobiles by the same name. Wrong. It was nothing more than a post office and a tiny collection of dilapidated houses on a dry, brown prairie. While that wasn't a hallucination, just an error of ignorance, what I saw next was a little closer to the twilight zone.

Several minutes after passing the post office, I came upon a woman walking. I slowed down to greet her and share a few words.

"How are you today?" I asked in my friendliest voice.

"Fine." She barely hid her annoyance at being forced to talk, but seemed to feel guilty at being so curt. "Just headed up to the post office," she added.

With that, she seemed satisfied that she had fulfilled her conversational obligation and started walking. In the brief moment she stopped, I got a look at her outfit. She was dressed in plaid cargo shorts which revealed mismatched knee socks and beat up loafers. She wore a down vest over a cotton t-shirt with a paisley scarf around her neck. Her hair was up in large rollers.

Upon closer inspection, the rollers were actually frozen orange juice cans.

The eccentricity of the outfit made me think of one thing: Rosemary.

In her later years, as the cheese slipped further off her cracker, Mama started to dress and act more outrageously. In her sixties, she insisted on getting breast augmentation, which she called her *boobery* job. The oversized hooters looked ridiculously out of proportion on her skeletal smoker's frame. My brother and I called her "Tits on a stick." She was fond of attending plays at the local Chattanooga playhouse dressed in costume. Once, the ticket taker, who was familiar with his odd customer, noticed that she had forgotten something important; her false teeth.

"Good evening, Rosemary, you look lovely tonight, but it looks like you forgot your teeth."

"It's part of my outfit," she gummed without missing a beat, and strolled right in.

My thoughts were with Mama as I rode away from the woman with orange juice rollers. I turned around to get one more look at her but she was gone. Maybe she went inside the post office. Maybe she was a figment of my exhausted imagination. I didn't bother to turn back to find out.

The ghost town of Bannack was the terminus of the day's strange trip. In 1862, nearby Grasshopper Creek was the site of the area's first gold rush, and Bannack even became the capital of Montana for a short while, boasting a population of 10,000 at its peak. Today, dozens of empty buildings (a hotel, houses, a school) bear silent witness of Bannack's short-lived turn at glory.

I arrived at the state park campground near the ghost town around 4 p.m. I had a lot of daylight left, but was just too tired to go on. I wanted nothing more than to pass out on my nice inflatable air mattress. The mosquitoes were horrendous. I quickly set up camp so that I could have the shelter of my tent. After erecting the tent, I dug in the Sweet Roll for my air mattress.

It wasn't there.

That's weird, I always put it here.

Although I never deviated from my packing arrangement, I rummaged through my other bags. Not there.

Then it dawned on me. On the descent into Helena several days before, I had rushed to get my puffy hoodie out of the bag in a driving rain. In my haste to minimize my exposure, I had forgotten to close the Sweet Roll. Somewhere along the way, the air mattress must have worked its way out of the bag.

Shit.

I lost my beloved flip flops on the first day, and now I had lost an even more important piece of gear. I wondered if I would have anything left by the time I reached the Mexican border.

CHAPTER 19

They say luck favors those who are prepared, but sometimes it throws a bone to knuckleheads, too. The loss of my air mattress should have been a serious blow to my rest, and therefore my race. In my preparations for the TD, I made a commitment to not cheat my rest time. Burning the candle at both ends might be possible in a shorter race, but over the course of hundreds of miles, and weeks on end, the hours would add up, the fatigue would add up, and the chances of dropping out would increase exponentially with each day. Some of these young bucks were able to take that sort of punishment, but most could not. An old lady in her fifties? Forget about it. I needed my sleep. So far, the investment had paid off. Although I was steadily losing time to the sleep-deprived superhumans in this race, I was still racing. I attributed much of this to my strict observance of the principles of sleep hygiene.

Thankfully, my campsite was covered in a thick layer of pea gravel, which had just enough pliability to give it the remotest qualities of a mattress—the world's hardest mattress for sure—but better than inflexible, packed dirt. As I lay on the ground, I swished my butt back and forth to dig a little hole to keep my back from arching uncomfortably, then placed my puffy hoodie under my hips for a bit more cushion, and slept soundly.

Better than soundly, actually. I awakened refreshed. The fatigue that had been accumulating since the beginning of the race had nearly vanished. I wondered if I had discovered some new sleep breakthrough.

Forget your steel coils, air, and memory foam. The hot new trend in mattress technology is pea gravel!

I didn't waste time trying to unravel the mysteries of the pea gravel miracle or outline a business plan to capitalize on the benefits of sleeping on a bed of rocks. My patent for a new mattress, and the fortune I would certainly make from it, would have to wait. It was a beautiful day and the mountains beckoned. It would be a shame to waste such a perfect day on something as mundane as becoming a multi-millionaire.

Despite my flippancy, money—or the lack of it—was always in the back of my mind. I had a schizophrenic relationship to it, alternating between obsession and disinterest. Basically, I would fret over money until I had an opportunity to ride, then I would forget all about it. In many ways, a bike was like a needle full of heroin to me. It made me forget the pain and embarrassment of my failure to create anything resembling a career and build a lifestyle similar to those I enviously witnessed all around me. My lack of any kind of normal job meant that I would always hunger for money, but my love affair with riding a bike was more powerful than the appeal of a regular paycheck and the drudgery that went with it. I suppose it never was much of a choice, really. It was how I was made. The coursing high of endorphins created when riding whisked the cobwebs of depression and shame from my mind even as they deadened the physical pain of effort and created a state that approached euphoria. What a wonder drug! A tiny molecule that helps a person forget the worst parts of life and makes that person feel alive and well. How could the pride-inflating properties of a career (and all the antidepressant drugs that a career's money could buy) begin to compare with that?

Unfortunately, endorphins don't pay the bills or put food on the table. Worse still, the good feelings are only temporary. The sadness is never eradicated, only banished for a while. Once the spent ashes of endorphins are carried by blood to some distant organ to be eliminated, the strings and dust of gloom gather in the corners once more, whispering malignantly, telling me I'm no good, worthless, a loser.

Thankfully, I was able to race the Tour Divide without much financial worry. A drug company that made a treatment for MS sponsored afflicted athletes for outreach and advertising. The drug company that sponsored me had originally committed to support me for the first two weeks, but agreed to continue until the end of the race. If it hadn't been for them, I would have been sleeping in the tent and eating ramen every night. Instead, I was "moteling" it nearly every night, living in relative luxury (and sometimes actual luxury) compared to the average TD racer. I felt a little twinge of guilt each time I slipped between cool sheets and sank blissfully into an actual mattress, but not nearly enough to resolve to live a more spartan lifestyle. After all, there were no rules regarding *where* a racer could stay. I justified my swanky accommodations with the rationale that comfort at night would translate to stamina during the days and weeks. In this game, finishing within the prescribed rules was the only thing that mattered.

The rules that govern the Tour Divide are pretty simple; a participant is to ride 100% of the race route end to end, and do so with only the support that she is able to provide for herself. In other words, a buddy with an RV can't offer a racer a place to sleep, even if he just happens to be camping along the way. Nor are friends allowed to meet a rider and give her food. All the support that a racer acquires must be commercially available to any racer. There are a few exceptions to this rule for emergency or replacement items, so I was legally able to call home and ask my friend Fischer to send me a replacement for my lost air mattress.

As I pedaled out of Bannack, I ruminated on the TD rules. The old Paul Simon tune *Fifty Ways to Leave Your Lover* played on repeat in my brain. To pass the time, I tried to come up with *Fifty Ways to Cheat the TD.* All the different ways to receive outside support would be an easy cheat, but advancing myself down the course by something other than my own power would be much more difficult because of the GPS spot tracker that not only recorded my position, but also my speed. For example, if a nice rancher offered to take me 20 miles ahead in his pickup truck, my spot tracker would record me going much faster than possible by pedaling alone, unless the rancher was willing to drive at about five miles an hour.

I could think of no way to effectively cheat the GPS that didn't involve convincing someone else to move it at the glacial pace achieved by a fifty-seven-year-old woman riding a fully loaded bicycle over uneven terrain. I was reminded of the HL Mencken quote, "Conscience is the little voice in our heads that warns us someone might be watching." Along with my internal conscience, which remained intact, the spot tracker was my external conscience, the eyes that watched—and transmitted—my doings. If ever I felt an overwhelming desire to find an expedited and unsanctioned way to the end this odyssey, the GPS would be there whispering in my ear, "Someone is watching."

The exercise in figuring out how to cheat had been an enjoyable way to pass the time, but I realized that I didn't even want to cheat. I had scrupulously adhered to the rules out of a sense of pride.

Eyes on the prize.

Finishing the race would be one victory. Finishing it honestly would be another. I wanted two wins, two weapons to fight the demons who constantly told me I was nothing.

The previous night, as I was setting up my tent, physically drained yet with still enough mental battery life to dread the pea gravel that awaited, a nearby camper came over to chat. Funny thing about people in campsites; they generally love to interact with a stranger and are not shy about approaching one. Something about sharing the limited space of a campground breaks down all the normal barriers of human interaction. There seems to be a sense among campers that the time spent camping is too rare and precious, so there is no time to waste on social formalities. There is an unwritten, yet understood, bond of instant friendship.

It was in this spirit that Steve strolled over to my site bearing a large plate of his "famous" macaroni salad. He chuckled at the deceptively self-deprecating use of the word famous. No doubt, when he showed up at the neighborhood cookout in Bison's Breath, Montana (or wherever he lived) carrying a big bowl of the salad, it drew exclamations of excitement and gratitude from all who attended. The thought of the scene charmed me, as did Steve's easy-going demeanor.

I imagined all the scenarios back in the "real" world in which a stranger offering a plate of undocumented food would be cause for skepticism and rejection, but out here in the unvarnished wild, sharing food seemed the most natural thing in the world. I eagerly accepted the macaroni and dug in, expressing my gratitude for the trail magic and confirming to Steve that his dish deserved to be called famous.

While I shoveled macaroni into my mouth, Steve gave me a scouting report for the next section of trail. A few miles out of town, he told me I would encounter a section of the road that would get my attention.

"So, uh, Grace, tomorrow you will be hitting Bannack Road. The mud is so thick there, you won't be able to ride it."

I snorted skeptically through a mouthful of food.

"No, seriously, it's really bad. You might want to pick up your bike and carry it."

I didn't want to seem rude, especially since he had given me food, so I nodded and acted like I was heeding his warning, but inside I was thinking, *He doesn't know how awesome I am at riding a bike.*

As predicted, the mud was there waiting for me, but it wasn't nearly as bad as reported. I scoffed at the report I received last night.

Ha, what does Macaroni Steve know about mud? This isn't anything compared to the mud back in Canada, much less Appalachian mud.

Ah, famous last words. The mud got progressively thicker until I was convinced that I had ridden into quicksand. It caked my drivetrain and the spaces between wheels and frame, and hardened into a concrete-like substance. Riding became impossible. I remembered Steve's suggestion about carrying the bike and now regretted dismissing it. I had to abandon the road and walk my bike along an equally muddy cow path that included cow pies and tumbleweed. There was no escape from the misery. The peanut buttery muck sloshed and stuck to everything it touched. As I walked, pickup trucks roared by. The drivers had to build up a head of steam to make it through the obstacle, and they sprayed brown rooster tails of mud that reminded me of the wake of a speedboat skimming across water.

The mud walk lasted about two miles. After I had passed it, I had to spend a ridiculous amount of time cleaning the gunk out of my bike to make it rideable again. I would be chiseling it off the frame for hundreds of miles, the last of it tenaciously hanging on well into Colorado.

I rolled into little Lima (pop. 277) to spend my last night in Montana. It had been another eighty-mile day. I was tired, but not exhausted. Something felt different, like my body had undergone some kind of metamorphosis. I was no longer wiped out at the end of the day. A new energy coursed through me like water from an inexhaustible spring. Maybe the pea gravel miracle really was a miracle.

CHAPTER 20

The ride out of Lima took me directly eastward toward Idaho, which sounds like a geographical error, seeing as how Idaho generally lies to the west of Montana. I checked my map to make sure I wasn't going the wrong way, and wouldn't end up in Seattle or Sioux Falls. Sure enough, the undulating Continental Divide, which forms this part of the border between the two states, gives Idaho a small north-ward-thrusting finger that sits to the east of the last miles of trail in this remote corner of Montana.

The day was like a vacation. The race up until this point had been a draining combination of rain, mud, snow, cold, sickness, fear, dog attacks, lost gear, and fatigue. It had been a multi-week gauntlet, a trial that seemed to be sent by angry gods to test my worthiness to be called a TD racer.

But where the misery had been spread more or less evenly over the last two weeks, the perfection of this day spilled its gifts over me extravagantly, as if Mother Nature had saved up to give me one spotless, shining day. The sun shone warmly on my back. A glorious tailwind pushed me gently for seventy-five miles. The snow-flecked caps of the Centennial Mountains rose serenely to the south as I pedaled through the relatively flat basin of the same name. The bright green prairie was spotted with deep blue ponds against a backdrop of treeless hills rolling to the north. Stands of dark conifers interrupted the visual silence of the prairie. Looking at the landscape, the words *Big Sky* leapt spontaneously into my brain. One of Montana's nicknames is Big Sky. It is a brilliant two-word distillation of the state's essence. The sublime scene rendered further description unnecessary and left me nearly speechless to even try.

I made my way through the Red Rock Lake Wildlife Refuge, which was established to preserve the endangered trumpeter swan, a stunningly beautiful animal with an eight-foot wingspan that's thirty pounds when fully grown. The swan population was down to one hundred animals before creation of the reserve back in the 1930s. Now, they number in the thousands.

Two swans took an interest in the strange animal riding a wheeled contraption. They stared at me as if they were trying to remember my name.

"Hello, John. Hello, Mikey," I said, nodding respectfully toward them.

Along with the swans, I saw a tree full of Bald eagles, and a massive moose standing in a shallow lake. Unlike my preparations for Grizzlies, I had done no scouting of the moose. I wish I had. Its sheer size was intimidating, and my ignorance of its habits and level of aggressiveness made me uneasy. He raised his huge antlered head and turned it toward me. I rolled on by without taking a photo, hoping not to provoke any ill feelings in the giant.

The day was full of my first sightings of exotic animals. Perhaps the most exotic of all was my first encounter with Tour Divide "Northbounders." The TD is a most unusual race. In addition to having no fixed start time, it also has two starting points. Traditionally, racers start at Banff and work south, but a few non-conformists choose to start at the Mexican border and ride north. I met a few of these rebels on this day, which just added to the pleasure.

One of the racers was a proud Belgian. Belgium is a cycling-mad country. The tiny nation produced the greatest cyclist of all time, Eddy Merckx, and the entire country embraces the bicycle with a fervor unmatched anywhere in the world. My new Belgian friend was a character. He wore a jersey patterned with the black, yellow, and red stripes of his country's flag. His rear rack was precariously stacked with gear, including a two-gallon plastic water jug. Flags were tied or duct taped to every available surface. A large Colorado state flag stuck out of the jumbled pile of gear on an actual wooden flag pole. The whole scene was one of incongruity and excess, a weird mash-up of Beverly Hillbillies-meets-European cyclist. Whereas I had tried to minimize weight and simplify my journey to the bare bones, this rider reveled in extravagance, unbothered by the dominant bikepacking philosophy of traveling light.

After visiting a bit and taking selfies, the Belgian untied one of his flags and presented it to me as a gift. I tied it to my bike and proudly flew the flag of Belgium on the rest of my journey through the heart of America.

The day included one CD crossing at Red Rock Pass. Before I reached the pass, I crossed Hell Roaring Creek, an otherwise ordinary stream that has the distinction of being the most distant source of the Missouri River. It was a pleasant thought to consider the water in this little creek would eventually find its way out of the mountains, crossing the vastness of the Great Plains, passing the arch in St. Louis, pulsing through New Orleans and the Louisiana bayou, and finally to the Gulf of Mexico, thousands of miles and millions upon millions of gallons later. Lewis and Clark were keen to mark the identity of this "most distant fountain," but incorrectly gave the title to another stream near Bannack.

The Red Rock Pass marked the end of my long journey through Montana. A sign proclaiming *Welcome to Idaho* marked the state line, the continental divide, and the start of a long descent into the next trail town and my bed for the night.

It had been a wonderful day. I had no idea what this day meant in the larger picture of the whole race. Did I just complete some kind of initiation rite into the brotherhood of long-distance athletes? Had my body completed a reorganization to meet the physical demands of massive daily effort? Would it be easier from here on out, or was it a respite between the hellish past and an unseen hell yet to come? Or was it just a random day, a metaphor for a life that gives tests and rests at such baffling intervals as to make a pattern indecipherable? It is this quest for pattern and predictability that both drives and frustrates us. We have become impatient strangers to mystery, uneasy in its unfamiliar presence, too hurried and ambitious to just let life unfold naturally. As I lay my head on the pillow, I began to see my life as a knot caused by this compulsion to strive. To control. To *know*. The strings of competing desires and expectations, tied by many people along the way, including myself, have all been attempts to divine and control patterns, and thus, life itself. I imagined that everyone had their own knot, but only I could untie this one. The days I had spent alone in the wilderness had given me the space to recognize it. Now I could work on undoing it. As I drifted to sleep, I had one final thought.

A big ass Colorado flag on an actual flag pole, for chrissakes. What will I see next?

CHAPTER 21

I awakened at an inn (what, me camp?) in the shadow of Sawtell Peak, a mountain that forms part of the rim of the massive Island Park caldera that is related to the the hyperactive Yellowstone caldera just across the border in Wyoming. I was in volcano country. Yellowstone famously oozes, bubbles, and spews thermal energy from its geysers, mud pots, and hot springs, evidence of a churning, seething monster below. The Island Park caldera where I bunked the night before was the old and sleeping grandfather of Yellowstone. Some 2.1 million years ago, gramps was sowing his wild oats, ejaculating with enough force to spread ash from Los Angeles to St. Louis. It is interesting that the area's calderas are on something of a 600,000-year eruption cycle. The last eruption was just over... wait for it...600,000 years ago. We are overdue for another big one. I hoped to be long gone from the area before any extinction-level geological fireworks commenced, but considering the destruction and worldwide famine that would result from such an eruption, it might be better to be standing on top of it when it blows.

As a source of peril, exploding volcanoes posed nowhere near the immediate threat as did the friggin' mosquitoes. The relentlessly attacking little buggers unnerved me. They were everywhere and they were vicious, like piranhas in air, stripping the meat from my bones one itchy needle prick at a time. Thousands upon thousands of them.

When I pedaled out of Banff, which seemed like a lifetime ago, I had a little travel size container of insect repellant, laughably thinking that it would last me the whole trip. It was now empty and the mosquitoes were growing demonically ravenous. Before leaving town, I purchased a mega-sized can of bug repellant—weight be damned—and doused myself.

The ride out of Island Park took me along a trail that was once a railroad bed. The Yellowstone Branch Line was built more than one hundred years ago and was the original route for tourists to get to America's first national park. The rail line was abandoned and eventually developed into what is known as a rail-trail. A national organization called the Rails-to-Trails Conservancy helps turn defunct rail lines into car-free trails for bike riding or pedestrian use. Since 1986, they have helped build some 32,000 miles of trails. Someday, they hope to connect the entire country in a network of car-free trails. I want to ride all of them.

Rail-trail sounds like the perfect place to ride a bike. It would have been except for one thing. This trail was in the fallout zone of one of those famous 600,000-year caldera eruptions and was covered in a thick layer of volcanic sand. It was like riding on a beach. For two hours, I struggled through the pillowy sand. To make matters worse, a parallel gravel road, mere feet away from the official race route, taunted me to come ride its hard-packed surface. My commitment to remain faithful to the TD rules was sorely tested.

The scenery of the Warm River Canyon somewhat made up for the tedious riding. I rode on a ledge overhanging the deep, narrow gash with crashing white water at the bottom. Climbing out of the canyon, I decided to take a rest stop at the Warm River Campground.

The campground was covered with campers. After so much solitude, any size gathering of people made me feel as if I had been dropped in Times Square, though this was more like Disney World, with kids running about and adults visiting their temporary neighbors, sharing stories and camp gossip. I soft-pedaled right down the main street of the campground collecting odd glances from people who were unfamiliar with the world of bikepacking. One of these curious campers strolled up to me, coffee cup in hand, and asked, "What's this rig?"

I gave him a quick class on bikepacking and told him of the Tour Divide and my itinerary which would take me from Banff to the Mexican border. He gave me that look of open-mouthed astonishment I had come to expect any time I told the story of what I was doing.

As we talked, the camp host walked into our conversation and asked, "Are you Grace?"

Coffee Boy was floored. "You know her?"

The camp host explained to Coffee Boy that he was a TD Dot Watcher and had been monitoring my progress as I neared his location. He then shooed Coffee Boy away and turned to me. He had a grandfatherly demeanor, and his pants were held up by both suspenders *and* a belt. I surmised that this was a man who didn't take chances.

"Grace, I pulled some trout out of the river this morning, how would you like me to fry some up for you?"

I ate the trout in the shade of a juniper tree while I watched kids play, grateful for trail magic and another perfect moment.

With my belly full of trout, I climbed out of the Warm River Canyon onto a flat plain. The abrupt transition between mountainous terrain and featureless prairie was discombobulating. It made me feel as if I had been transported by some futuristic technology hundreds of miles away. As I made my way east toward my stop for the night, I could see the legendary Teton Range to the southeast. This much-photographed mountain range was perhaps the most famous in America, and I would have a front row seat to its majesty for the rest of the day and much of tomorrow.

Chapter 22

The rest of the day was spent between the two giants, Yellowstone and Grand Teton National Parks. I briefly touched Yellowstone's border but could see none of its well-known thermal features. It just looked like a typical Rocky Mountain forest. Its secrets and wonders lay far north. The Tetons, on the other hand, loomed stately to the south. It was a view that never got old.

My lodging for the night at Flagg Ranch benefited tremendously from its position between the two parks. The enterprising owners took full advantage of their prime location and were able to command $300 per night for their accommodations. The outlay of $200 for the swanky room in Whitefish made me blush, but this place took the cake. The drug company funding this adventure had a generous cap of $200 per night, so I would have to make up the $100 difference out of my own pocket. Or camp.

I shelled out the $100 and trudged toward my cabin. I might not win the Tour Divide, but if there was a prize for softest racer, I would surely win it going away. If the TD had a yearbook, I would be voted "Most likely to stay in a motel."

To top it off, my $300 room wasn't even luxurious. To be more accurate, it didn't even rise to the level of mediocre. The place had apparently been built shortly after Lewis and Clark surveyed the area. It had no TV or WiFi. It did have electricity in the form of a single light dangling from the ceiling. I also had roommates. Lots and lots of roommates. They were small and black and annoying. They flew. They buzzed in my ears and sucked my blood all night.

I couldn't wait to get out of the place the next morning. Mostly I wanted to escape the ubiquitous mosquitoes, but I was also excited to be riding with a view of the Tetons for much of the day.

The Tetons were named *Les Trois Tetons* by early French explorers. The name literally means *the three tits*, so it is safe to assume the French were probably snickering college frat boys trying to find a keg party when they first saw the mountains.

The Teton range is the youngest in the entire Rockies at 'only' six to nine million years old. Its jagged peaks shoot directly off the valley floor like sharp-nosed rockets piercing the sky. There are no buffering foothills to dilute the view. This gives the mountains an immediate, in-your-face grandeur that defies the viewer to look away.

I happily became a tourist for a few hours as the TD route took me along the main road of the park. I feasted my eyes on the peaks Moran, Bivouac, Eagles Rest, and the signature Teton triplets, as minivans, RVs, and sedans whooshed by. By the time I reached my turnoff, I had my fill of automobiles and longed to return to the quiet of the car-free world, Tetons or no Tetons.

I turned to the east and ascended Buffalo Valley Road to the 9,600 ft. CD pass at Togwotee. It was cold and cloudy at the top of the pass, so I put on my jacket before heading down the mountain. Once again, the joy of descending overcame my sense of responsibility to look at the map and I missed a turn.

Shit.

Missing a turn always put me into a surly mood. The thought of backtracking unnecessarily was infuriating. It didn't help that the correct route was a snowy, muddy path instead of a smoothly paved highway.

After sixty-nine miles and 5,000 ft. of climbing, I arrived at my bed for the night. It was a "camper cabin," with two wooden bunks and a small table. There was no heat and no bathroom, but it did have a foam mattress. Since I was still without my air mattress, this amenity more than made up for the lack of others. I walked across the compound to the bath house. The shower required quarters to operate and didn't supply towels. My decision to forego the added weight of vending machine money and the bulk of a terry cloth towel seemed like a no-brainer back in Banff. Now I was paying for my monk-like simplicity. I had little choice but to "go hog" and sleep dirty in my bag.

CHAPTER 23

It probably goes without saying, but most people generally sleep better when clean than they do dirty. I was no exception to this rule and certainly had no desire to relinquish my self-awarded title of "softest TD racer." Nor did I like the feeling of waking up covered in sticky sweat and putting dirty clothes back on, but that's what I did.

In this disgusting state, I shuffled across the road to a convenience store & restaurant. The cashier informed me the restaurant would not open for another hour, so I had to settle for coffee. I could hear a voice coming from the darkened restaurant. It was the sound of a man talking loudly to himself in what sounded like the amped-up enthusiasm of a radio voice.

"What's going on in there?" I asked the cashier.

"Radio station from James Town is doing a live remote. He's looking for people to interview, would you like to talk with him? If you do, the coffee's on the house."

He said the magic word—*free*. If it had been a TV interview, I would've had to pass. I looked, and probably smelled, as bad as a drunk at the end of a three-day bender. But nobody could see this train wreck on radio, so I agreed. My segment was wedged between interviews with a fresh-faced rodeo cowboy and a weather-beaten rancher. While I was waiting for my spot, I recalled my training as an MS spokesperson. The drug company that sponsored me had sent me to classes to learn how to give interviews.

Take control of the interview. Get to the point quickly. Remember the bottom line.

I gave the host my elevator speech about the Tour Divide. For a small town disc jockey, the guy was a pro. He asked thoughtful questions and we had a nice chat. Near the end of my interview,

I mentioned that I had MS. His mouth dropped open. During the commercials he said he couldn't leave it hanging like that and asked if I could stay for another segment. I obliged and we had another nice conversation. When he asked how I could do such demanding races with MS, I responded that I didn't consider what I was doing to be extraordinary. I was just living my life like my mother told me to decades ago.

Good ol' Rosemary. Nearly forty years later, her advice was still guiding me. After the interview, I got my free coffee at the register and bolted out the door. The interview had cost me forty-five valuable minutes. I had to stop myself from becoming anxious about the lost time. I reminded myself that although this was technically a race, it wasn't *that* kind of race. Forty-five minutes would not make a difference when my finishing time would be measured in weeks.

The climb up Union Pass, the second consecutive 9,000-footer, took about five hours of relentless climbing. Once at the top, the trail stayed around the 9,000 ft. level for many miles. This was my first extended encounter at high elevation and I was on alert for the signs of altitude sickness: fatigue, headache, nausea, and shortness of breath. Thankfully, nothing happened and I was able to motor on to a big two-mile downhill that took me into the remote Green River valley. I was warned (again) to be on the lookout for Grizzlies. This meant more atrocious singing and butchered nursery rhymes, but I didn't see any bears.

I made good enough time that I was able to push on to the town of Pinedale, Wyoming. Besides the obvious pull of a comfortable motel bed, I had another big reason to get there. Fischer, my buddy back in Huntsville, had called REI and ordered a replacement for the one that now sat alone on a mountainside somewhere back in Montana. The mattress was scheduled to be delivered to the post office in Pinedale.

I made it to the post office just before closing. The mattress was not there. Although it wasn't a disaster, I had a small shudder of panic; the kind of panic you have when you're running late and can't find your keys. Something is supposed to be there, but it isn't. I could feel the anxiety welling up. I made a call to Fischer, hoping to reach him. He answered.

Fischer had been unable to get the same kind of mattress I had lost. The adhesive that came with the repair kit was apparently so toxic that it was banned from all methods of shipping. Fischer had to order a substitute mattress that could be shipped, and even then, it was not allowed by the post office. So, he had to FedEx the mattress to a motel in Pinedale. I pedaled over to the motel to retrieve my package and book a room.

This mattress was big, much bigger than the original. And heavy. The brand name of this monstrosity was Big Agnes. I decided to inflate it to see how it worked. The thing was so big, it took forty-five minutes to inflate.

That's not going to work when it's late and I'm tired.

Once inflated, it took up the entire floor of the tent. It also took up too much room in the Sweet Roll, requiring me to reallocate gear to other bags.

Big Agnes, my ass. I'm going to call you Morbidly Obese Agnes.

I was stuck with the mattress for the time being, but made a mental note to change it out when I ran across an REI, which would probably be several days away in Silverthorne, Colorado.

CHAPTER 24

The next morning while I was eating the motel's complimentary breakfast, I received a text from Dawson, who was watching my dot. It sounded urgent, *"TD rider Miles Parker is in Boulder. Catch him. You don't need to go through the Basin alone."*

Well, that sounded serious. First of all, I wasn't sure why "The Basin" was such a big deal, nor did I understand the significance of having a riding partner. Nevertheless, I knew Dawson was level-headed and wouldn't give frivolous advice. He had recently ridden the TD route and was acting as my virtual scout. Without hesitation, I left my leisurely breakfast and saddled up. As much as I enjoyed the unhurried aspects of this "race," it had started to feel more like a vacation. Dawson's directive had snapped me out of island time and back into race mode. I had purpose once again, the fire of an immediate goal that had to be tracked and slayed.

Boulder, Wyoming was some twelve miles from my hotel in Pinedale. Assuming this Miles Parker character was not laying over in Boulder, he wouldn't be there when I arrived, but somewhere down the course. I would have to ride hard to catch him before the day was through.

Ride hard I did. I "time trialed." In the bike racing world, a time trial is a kind of race where riders go out onto a course individually. Every few seconds another rider starts and races the clock. The hard thing about a time trial is that a rider has no reference point from which she can compare how well she is doing. In a regular race, where everyone starts at the same time, there are always other racers nearby from which one can judge one's position. There are even opportunities to "rest" in the slipstream of the pack. In a time trial, however, a racer is isolated in her own world of pain, racing flat out at the body's redline, not knowing if the time is good or bad until after the race is over, but always feeling that her fastest is not fast enough.

I flew along Highway 191 with my head down, pushing the pedals in a piston-like cadence, applying the power of muscle and bone to this marvelous machine. The physics of riding a bike (the numbers and equations that describe terms like force, velocity, mass, drag, gyroscopic effect, etc.) are impossibly complex and will forever remain unknowable to me. But the culmination of that invisible science—the beautiful act of a human riding a bike with strength, balance, and freedom—had become the thing through which I measured the value of my life. It was my essence.

As predicted, when I reached Boulder, Miles was gone. The good news was that I only had to go in one direction to find him. After refilling water bottles and getting a quick snack, I hopped back on the bike and continued my pursuit through the empty countryside. I rode atop the continental divide with sweeping views of the tumbled gray blocks of the Wind River Mountains to my north, the monochromatic, forbidding desert of the Great Divide Basin to the south, and the endless blue canopy above. The term that came to mind when looking at the vastness all around me was *lonely*. But *lonely* has a negative connotation, one that implies longing, incompleteness. At that moment, I did not long for anything. It was one of the most fulfilling times of my life. I especially did not need company, but I was about to get it.

I caught up with Miles. My time trial had been a success. He was sitting under a tree taking a snack break. He had removed his shoes and helmet. He looked to be about my age, with streaks of gray at his temples and a slight middle-age paunch protruding under his green cycling jersey. I put on my best cheerleader face and rode up to him to break the ice.

"Are you Miles Parker?" He didn't say anything. He just looked at me as if I was about to hand him a subpoena.

Awkward. I tried again.

"I'm Grace. You're in the Tour Divide, right?"

"Yes," he said.

"I was wondering if you would want to ride through the Basin together?" It was funny how ten minutes ago I was content to be alone, but now that I had made an offer of companionship, I desperately wanted it to be accepted. I felt like I had asked a boy to go to prom with me and waited in agony for an answer.

Miles' tongue finally loosened and he agreed to my suggestion. Thus, my first "trail marriage" was initiated. As we rode our first miles together, he told me he was an electrical engineer from Ohio. He talked (pontificated, really) about a number of subjects from bicycle gearing ratios to the geology of Wyoming, but never asked me any questions. I listened respectfully. We rode together into a town with the geographically confusing name of Atlantic City. There were no oceans or casinos in this Atlantic City. In fact, there wasn't much of anything. Its population, as listed on the town sign, was "about 57." Apparently, the townspeople were so laid back that they couldn't be bothered to count all fifty-seven and remained satisfied with an approximate census.

Our bunk for the night was at a bed and breakfast called Wild Bills. The wild west sounding name was more than apropos. Wild Bill had built an impressive collection of taxidermy and enough guns to kill every last animal in Wyoming. To complete the eccentricity of the dead zoo/gun store/bed and breakfast combo, Bill's wife was a damn good baker and gave us a slice of the best cherry pie I have ever tasted.

Miles and I walked across town (one block, actually) to eat dinner. Our waitress pegged us for TD racers and began talking as she tapped her order pad nervously with her pen.

"My son used to race motorcycles."

Which has absolutely nothing to do with a cross-country bicycle race.

I didn't want to appear rude, but I really just wanted her to take our order and bring us food, and lots of it. She pressed on.

"Yeah, but he don't no more. Wrecked his car and now he's paralyzed from the waist down."

I felt like a heel for being so selfish. She obviously needed to talk about the tragedy that visited her family, so I ignored my growling tummy and listened. She said her son was now trying to be a paraplegic wheelchair racer and she was saving tips to raise money for a proper racing chair. I told her about my disease and that my bike had been a grant from the Challenged Athletes Foundation. Her face lit up and she jotted down the name of the foundation. I was reminded of the power travel has to enhance our lives when we open our hearts. A simple, random interaction may have changed the trajectory of the lives of two strangers. I had been the recipient of so many of these random blessings on this adventure. It felt good to be on the giving end.

CHAPTER 25

Atlantic City marked the beginning of the Great Divide Basin. It also was a landmark in another incredibly significant way. It marked the end of Grizzly country. This mighty animal once ranged over two-thirds of the continent from Mexico to Alaska and California to Ohio. Now its empire is in ruins, diminished due to displacement by another, cleverer apex predator.

For nearly 1,400 miles, I had fretted about this beast. It haunted a year's worth of preparation, and every sleep, every pedal stroke, and nearly every thought since I left Banff. I was glad to be free of the fear that had gripped me for so long. A weight had been lifted, both figuratively and literally as I dropped the heavy bear spray canister in the donation box on Bill's porch. Some Northbounder would likely pick it up and carry it—and the fear of *Ursus horribilis*—back to Banff.

Miles and I might have been out of the woods with regard to bears. We were literally out of the woods as we left the forested mountains for the barren wasteland of the Basin. But we were certainly not out of the woods yet.

The Great Divide Basin is a hydrological anomaly. It is a 4,000 square mile desert where water does not flow east or west; a drainage dead zone that is not partitioned by the continental divide. The tiny amount of water that finds its way here is cursed to find neither the Atlantic nor the Pacific, but disappears into underground tombs or evaporates back into the air.

It is a hard place, forsaken by Mother Nature, inaccessible to human ambition. Wind scours the high plains, forbidding the dreams of man to take root. In the great migration of the 1800s, westbound settlers who courageously risked life every day on the Mormon and Oregon Trails did not tempt this desert. Even though the terrain was easier here than the surrounding mountains, they steered clear of this graveyard where water itself goes to die.

Dawson's warning now made sense to me. While there was physical danger here, primarily in the form of dehydration, there was something else. Something sinister lurked in the voided landscape, a psychological vampire poised to drain the sanity out of an unsuspecting soul. Just as water was sucked underground, this place threatened to draw a human spirit out of its body and into its dark chambers, leaving a desiccated ghost to wander among the sagebrush.

I was glad to have Miles with me. This haunted plain could transform a healthy love of solitude into maddening isolation. There were no carefree birds flitting between reassuring trees, no comforting sounds of gurgling creeks. All was wind and waste. Additionally, there was only one water source along today's hundred-mile route. To miss the spring could prove deadly. It was nice to have another traveler with me to stay alert for it.

We found the spring then continued to our stop for the night, the mid-desert settlement of Wamsutter. The only break from the monotonous miles was the sight of the wild horses that scratch out a living here. Before we caught a glimpse of the horses, we passed several large piles of what looked like horse poop.

"Hey Miles, what is that?" I asked.

"Shit if I know," he smirked, satisfied by his witty answer.

Without making any physical contact with the piles, we confirmed by smell that the piles were indeed made of feces.

"Who on earth would stack shit like that?" he wondered.

"Have you ever seen rock cairns along treeless trails?" I offered. "Maybe it's a poop cairn to keep riders on the right track." Miles snorted derisively at the suggestion but didn't offer any alternative explanations.

Actually, our poop cairns were made by the horses themselves. Male horses, eager to mark territory and show dominance, take turns shitting in the same place until a large mound, called a stud pile, is formed in a smelly display of one-upmanship. Boys are so dumb.

A couple of the wild ponies were standing alongside the path as we passed. They didn't look aggressive or curious. They just stood there and watched us go by as if we were long time neighbors riding by their house.

"Hey, John. Hey, Mikey," I said.

"Why did you call them John and Mikey?" Miles asked.

"Oh, no reason," I lied. That was a secret I would keep to myself.

The town of Wamsutter, Wyoming sits alongside Interstate 80 and serves the natural gas industry. It had a dusty, end-of-the-world feel to it. There was one truck stop, one restaurant, and one motel. Miles and I rolled into the truck stop feeling like lycra-clad aliens in this world of denim and diesel. We were looking for food to supply tomorrow's continued trek through the desert, and expected the usual assortment of processed, preserved, plastic-encased Frankenfood. I was delighted to find fresh fruit, like pineapple and watermelon. I changed my mind about the place. It was not a dead-end, it was an oasis. Miles and I felt like royalty surveying a feast as we looked at the stocked coolers and shelves.

Happy and reloaded, we rode to the other side of the interstate to our motel. A young couple had recently bought the motel with the idea of catering to cross-country cyclists. As we checked in, she asked if there was anything we needed. An irritated toe on my left foot had been on my mind for the past few days. It had become red and angry and had finally demanded attention. I asked her if she might have any Epsom salts. She disappeared and returned with a large bag of powder. "There you go," she chirped. I didn't really have room for any more gear, so I shoved it in the Ludicrous Food Bag.

The next day was more monotonous riding through the basin, but Miles and I were upbeat. On this day we would leave the desert and cross the border into Colorado. Colorado meant I was getting closer to one of the big carrots that propelled me to endure this odyssey. I would soon see my son. The thought of it both excited me and knotted my stomach with anxiety.

CHAPTER 26

Much as we try not to become our parents, nature persistently erodes our will and shapes us into something sickeningly familiar. We catch glimpses of them in the mirror, feel their words in our mouths, and their shadows in our movements. To become what we once despised is a slow, yet inexorable process. We like to think of ourselves as spotless and unique, blind to the truth that most of what we are is just recycled DNA. This fact of life was revealed to me most clearly when my son Wills became estranged from me just like I had once removed myself from Rosemary.

Wills was eleven years old when his father and I split. In that fragile time just before puberty, the rug was pulled from Wills' life. The destruction wrought by an ugly divorce took a heavy toll on him. The fallout from custody battles and the tumult of puberty made him angry and sullen. My sweet child slipped further from me with each teenage outburst. Once, during an argument, he said that I was as crazy as my mother. I slapped him in outrage. It had been a grave error, which his father used to drive a wedge between us. Our relationship deteriorated into sporadic, terse exchanges of texts. And then nothing at all. I wondered if Rosemary felt a similar heartbreak when I withdrew from her.

The last break between us came about five years ago when Wills was in his mid-twenties. I ran into him in a parking lot in Huntsville. He had let himself descend into video gamer shape, with potato chip flab and an unkempt neckbeard. He was sporting a tattoo. I lost my composure.

"Is that a fucking tattoo?" I spat those ill-considered words at him with a bias born of a lifetime of being taught tattoos were the identifying mark of the lower class. In my youth, I had been one step removed from that lower class myself. Economically speaking, as a divorcee without a career, I was solidly lower class. Yet all the years of being groomed for Chattanooga society left a residue that had persisted for decades. In my upbringing, a tattoo was one of those disadvantages that only a fool would inflict upon himself.

I was the fool. I had used my undisciplined tongue like a whip against my child and pushed him completely away over a harmless tattoo. I learned a few weeks later that Wills was moving to Breckenridge, Colorado. My chances to patch things up with him would be diminished even further with a thousand miles between us. I was crushed.

I had texted Wills before starting the race to let him know I would be riding through Breckenridge and hoped to see him. He responded with a brusque, "O.K." Those two letters gave me hope...and heartburn.

The scenes of bruised love and lost time replayed in my mind as I climbed absentmindedly out of the Wyoming desert and into the aspen-lined trails of Colorado. Lost in daydreams, fueled by adrenaline produced from hurtful memories of my broken relationship, I left Miles far behind to struggle on his own up the fifteen-mile climb. My reverie was eventually interrupted by the sound of cowbells. As I rounded a bend, the source of the bells was revealed. It wasn't a cow. I had arrived at Brush Mountain Lodge.

Kirsten, the proprietress of the lodge, was a legend among the bikepacking community. A dedicated dot watcher, she gave each racer a ringing welcome reminiscent of European bike races with their tradition of spectators ringing bells to celebrate and motivate racers. She practiced hospitality the way Michelangelo practiced art. She was a master.

"Grace!" she screamed like a long lost friend, "Welcome to Brush Mountain!"

She charged me with arms wide open and wrapped me in a big hug.

"Drop your bike anywhere and relax on the deck. I'll have your pizza out in a minute."

Pizza? Can she read my mind?

I had been fantasizing about pizza for days. She fed me pizza, washed my clothes, and fed me more pizza. She even took the time to soak my damaged foot in the Epsom salts I had bummed from the Wamsutter motel. When Miles showed up, the process was repeated for him; bells, food, and all...minus the foot soaking. He was clearly uncomfortable with so much fuss being made for him. We sat in the cool evening air on the lodge's deck, eating Kirsten's scratch-made pizza, luxuriating in cotton clothes that she loaned us while ours were being washed. A starry sky completed the moment.

After the psychological test of the Basin, Brush Mountain Lodge was nirvana. Kirsten pampered me with service unlike any I had ever received. Her hospitality repaired my body and restored my spirit. The Basin drained energy. Kirsten replenished it with equal capacity. It was as if the universe placed her close to the Basin to balance its negative vibe with her boundless positivity.

Energy was what we needed. The Tour Divide route had bottomed out at the U.S.-Canada border around 2,500 ft. above sea level and had been steadily gaining altitude with every major pass. In Colorado we would hit the highest points of the race, soaring over 11,000-foot passes, testing our endurance and altitude tolerance.

Our mettle would be tested right off the bat with a long climb to the 10,000 ft. Watershed Divide, the highest yet. It was followed by a teeth-rattling descent off the mountain. All in all, we would descend more than 3,000 ft. over the course of thirty-three miles to the ski town of Steamboat Springs. It should have been an easy day.

It was not.

Despite the high elevation, it was hot. The scorching route offered little shade. There was nowhere to hide and nothing to do but keep going. I was glad this heat hadn't greeted us in the Basin. If it had, it might have altered everything.

We made it to the little settlement of Clark, which had a store and cafe. I had intended to make it a quick break, but Miles decided to order a hamburger. The heat continued to rise as I waited for him to finish. By the time we left, we had spent an hour in Clark. I had not intended to stay that long, but I made no protest. After all, that wouldn't have been ladylike.

Steamboat, the next town we came upon, might as well have been Disney World. Tourists jammed every corner of the town. I wanted nothing more than to get a quick snack and get out of town, but Miles needed to take his bike to the shop to get a few repairs. Another delay.

The heat pounded me as I waited on a bench outside the bike store. Then, out of nowhere, it hit me. Waves of fatigue rolled over me like an incoming tide. A tingly sensation radiated through my body. My vision blurred. Elvis said hello.

MS had followed me to Colorado.

I didn't tell Miles about my flare-up. After his bike was finished, we rode to a grocery store to resupply. The air-conditioned store was a godsend. Coolness is therapeutic for my MS symptoms, so I stood in front of the meat cooler and waited as the neurological fire drained out of my body.

Miles noticed my unusual delay and walked over to me.

"Is everything alright?"

"Yeah, I was just thinking about hamburgers," I said as I stared at pink mounds of ground chuck.

He snorted knowingly and walked away. It wasn't the taste of a hamburger I was dreaming of, but the hour that his hamburger had cost me back in Clark.

We eventually rode out of Steamboat. The MS scare had subsided but left me drained. The heat continued its assault. My goal was to make it to Lynx Pass to camp. The high pass would be cool overnight, which would help extinguish my symptoms.

We didn't make it.

We had lost too much time and I was too tired to make the hard push needed to reach the pass. As we realized this early in the evening, we began looking for places to camp. Unfortunately, we were passing through private ranchlands where camping was not allowed. The ranches were mostly populated by herds of sheep and tough sheepdogs. In my preparations, I had learned of the no-nonsense nature of the Great Pyrenees. These big dogs are all business and will defend their herds violently if they feel threatened. Thus, we did not want to trespass and run the risk of another dog attack.

Darkness was descending quickly and we were running out of options. Finally, we rode past a ranch with a "For Sale" sign planted out front. The place had no herd of grazing sheep and the big house on the hill looked empty, so Miles and I snuck past the gate and set up camp behind a little ridge to conceal our location from the road.

I was now a wild west outlaw, a desperado capable of violating settlers' property rights at will. If this lawless act was to be the beginning of a life of crime, it was evident to me right away that karma is always waiting to punish the wicked. For the sin of trespassing, I was kept awake all night by the sound of the neighbors' bleating sheep and barking dogs.

CHAPTER 27

The cops didn't show up to haul us off to jail overnight. Still, we didn't want to be witnessed by any passersby who might rat us out to the authorities, so shortly after dawn, we broke camp and made our way quickly back to the road. Despite the karmic retribution from the livestock the night before, we had gotten away with poaching a campsite on private property. Relief was my main emotion, but I couldn't help feeling a little exhilaration over the successful episode of breaking the law, however minor.

"Miles, we're outlaws now. We can never go back," I joked. Miles gave a courtesy smirk, but didn't answer. Humor was clearly not his thing.

As we made our way up to Lynx Pass, we passed a road sign that had a graphic of a sheepdog along with the words "Working Dogs. Not Friendly." The reminder couldn't have been more timely as we rounded a bend and rolled up to a herd of sheep blocking the road. A couple of hundred-pound Great Pyrenees bodyguards were close by, keeping a skeptical eye on us.

"Hello, John. Hello, Mikey," I said to them, hoping they would not misinterpret my greeting.

The herd was in no hurry to move. We didn't have a lot of options. Waiting in the searing sun was a sure recipe for a return of Elvis. Scaring the sheep into moving would have been literally suicidal. Turning back and rerouting was impossible.

We did the most logical, yet riskiest, thing we could. We dismounted the bikes and walked through the herd as non-threateningly as we could. If I hadn't been so frightened of provoking a response from the dogs, it would've been supremely satisfying to walk through the *baas* of the docile sheep. But as closely as we were being watched, the only thing I felt was stress.

It was like walking through a minefield, trying not to make a wrong move.

We made it safely through the herd and continued to Lynx Pass. A screaming downhill dropped us more than 2,000 ft. in just a few miles, taking us from the relative coolness of the spruce and aspen forests of the higher elevation, to the heat tolerant junipers and piñons of lower elevations. It was one of the most memorable and dangerous descents of the entire route: steep, fast, and rocky. One moment of inattentiveness could send a speeding rider sailing off the path and into eternity. My technical skills outpaced those of Miles, so I left him to work his way down, while I rocketed down the trail to the banks of the Colorado River.

This part of the legendary river was small and tranquil, a favorite with fishermen and rafters. It was remarkable to think that a few hundred miles downstream, this peaceful river would be responsible for the most majestic excavation project in history, the Grand Canyon.

I removed my shoes and sweat-soaked socks, and sat in the shade of a pavilion near the river. The heat was brutal again on this day. I could feel the shadow of MS creeping into my body again. I was so tired. All I wanted to do was set up camp next to the river and immerse myself in the cool water. But it would be foolish to ride wet (a sure recipe for chafing, blisters, and rashes), and we had only ridden about thirty miles so far. It was far too early to quit, although that was all I wanted to do.

"If I wasn't trying to get to Breckenridge, I would stop here for the day," I said as Miles rolled into the pavilion.

"Really?" He sensed I wasn't my usual gung-ho self. He was right, but I didn't tell him the reason for my fatigue.

After Miles rested a bit, we saddled back up. One truism of riding a bike—once you reach a river, there is nowhere to go but up—proved accurate once again as we climbed a dusty trail for miles. The difficulty of climbing, always exhausting in itself, was compounded by the heat. There were no groves of aspen to provide a bit of shade. The route was lined with stubby little scrub trees, leaving us completely exposed to the merciless sun.

Despite my impatience to make it to Breckenridge to see Wills, it soon became evident that I would have to wait. The day was too hot and the miles too hard, so we punted after making barely fifty miles. The little town of Kremmling sat two miles off the route. Two miles might not sound like much by car, but it is a significant detour by bike, especially in the heat. Normally, I wouldn't go so far out of the way, but I desperately wanted an air-conditioned refuge from the blazing sun. Other than its off-route location, Kremmling was exactly what we needed. It was a town that didn't share in the wealth and fame—or the crowds—of nearby ski towns, but it had a motel. It was a perfect place to rest, and escape the oppressive sun, and emotional heat of too many people.

Miles and I each rented a room. I went to mine and turned the air conditioning on high. I stripped naked and stood in front of it, freezing Elvis out of the room.

Chapter 28

It is about fifty miles from Kremmling to Breckenridge. No matter what obstacles stood in my way, I vowed that I would make it to Breck. The temperature cooperated with my mandate, moderating the blistering highs of the past couple of days that had melted me, and opened the door for an unwanted visit from MS. While thankful for the reprieve, it was not lost on me that I was heading south into the teeth of summer and the unforgiving desert heat of southern New Mexico.

That was a worry for another day. This was a day to celebrate. MS had subsided completely. I felt strong again. Miles and I made good time, even climbing over 9,500 ft. Ute Pass with little of the grousing that usually accompanies a long climb.

We entered the tourist haven of Silverthorne. The TD route joined a paved bike path that stretched from Silverthorne to Breckenridge, so the remainder of our day would be on a car-free paved road. It promised to be the easiest and most stress-free riding of the entire tour.

It would've been except for one detail we overlooked.

It was July 3rd. The town was stuffed with families enjoying the holiday break. The bike path was littered with old men on recumbent bikes, bros on mountain bikes, kids on BMX bikes, and dads and moms on bikes pulling trailers full of little crumb-crunchers. The oddity of our loaded bikepacking rigs added to the eccentricity of the collection. We weaved through the slow-rolling horde, gathering puzzled looks from the tourists. We had to stop for a red light in Frisco. A family rolled up next to us. The son, a boy of about eight, was fascinated by our packed bikes and asked what we were doing.

"We are riding to Mexico," I said.

I'm sure that he didn't grasp the magnitude of how far Mexico was from Frisco, but his mouth flew open all the same. His parents had a much better handle on the massive distance that stood between us and our goal and wore the same facial expression.

As my marriage began to disintegrate in the late nineties, I looked for ways to stay involved in my son's life. I organized a boys' mountain bike club for Wills and his friends. I first took them on day-long outings to local trails, and then on weekend trips to the mountains of North Carolina. Wills' best friend, Jack, took a liking to the mountain bike life which eventually led him to Colorado and a gig as a bike shop mechanic in Breckenridge. Over the years, Jack and I kept in touch even as my communication with Wills slowed to a trickle. Jack had since moved to Denver, but he still had contacts in Breck and helped with arrangements to have my bike serviced at his old store.

When I rolled up to the bike shop, Jack was there waiting on me! It was such a pleasant surprise. He had taken the day off and traveled from Denver to Breckenridge just to see me. I hugged him hard and fought back tears. He grabbed my bike.

"What does your bike need?" he asked.

"Wash it," I said. The mud from Bannack Road back in Montana was still hanging on.

As Jack disappeared with my bike, I called to him, "Where's Wills?"

Jack smiled and said, "He should be here any time."

While I rested, more surprises walked in the door. Two friends, Jamie and Justin, came all the way from Alabama to intercept me. Jamie had flown while Justin drove his van. It was becoming a Huntsville reunion.

Then another man rode his bike up to the store and walked in. He was tall and fit with a neatly trimmed beard and blue eyes that reminded me of Lake Louise in Banff.

It was my baby. My Wills.

Tears flooded my eyes as he walked toward me with a noticeable limp.

I threw myself at him, and cried the tears only a mother can. In that moment, 1,000 miles from the finish line, my Tour Divide was complete. Through all the mud, the miles, the pain, the cold, the darkness, the rain, the fear, and the exhaustion, this was why I was here. I was holding my son once more.

"How are you doing, Mom?"

"What happened to your leg?" I asked.

"Broke my tib-fib skiing last year."

"Your tibia *and* fibula? Last year? Nobody told me."

"I know. I didn't want you to worry. I'm fine."

My heart was broken again. My baby had suffered a serious injury and I had no clue. The realization that I was a non-entity in Wills' life burned. I felt betrayal for not being told, jealousy for his father who surely knew, and anger that his dad would keep it from me. I also felt like an utter failure at parenting. I had a quick choice to make. I could vent my righteous indignation or swallow my pride.

The old Grace would've stuck to her guns and held on to her grievance. The old Grace would've said something inflammatory and ruined this perfect moment.

The new Grace paused. I studied his face while my heart made up its mind. It was the face I had given birth to, the face that belonged to the soul I loved like no other.

I hugged him again and buried all the pain of the past in his present embrace. This was no time to litigate past crimes, it was a time to release and rejoice. I wasn't just reuniting with my son, I was reconciling.

Someone produced a cold case of Budweiser. The words *Go Grace* were written on the cans with a Sharpie. A party erupted. As we drank beer and relaxed, Jack tuned my bike, replacing the worn chain and installing two new tires. I told story after story of my adventures so far. My Chinese grandma. The Black Trail. The rain. The cold. The bugs. The bear. The fear. The wonder.

With each tale, I could see a glimmer of pride in Wills' eyes. His old lady was a badass.

After the impromptu party and dinner, Justin drove Miles and me back to Silverthorne, where we had reservations to spend the night. Before retiring for the evening, I went to REI to exchange Morbidly Obese Agnes for a more svelte air mattress.

Miles and I had been allowed to store our bikes at the shop in Breckenridge overnight. What a strange feeling it was to drive away without it. The bike had become more than a machine, more than an inanimate object. It was my constant companion, a reliable friend with the gift of silence. Like an infant, I had to provide 100% of its care and had never been more than a few feet away from it for more than four weeks. While it was nice to have a break from the responsibility, I also felt a little naked and lost without it.

As I lay my head on the pillow that night, I lingered over the scenes from this perfect day. It had unfolded like a fantasy I dared not indulge in the days prior. I began my day riding a bike in the warm sun of Colorado, surrounded by mountains, free of all earthly burdens but one. I ended the day with even that one lifted. Liberated. Healed of the years of torture that I had inflicted on myself for the sin of being imperfect; made whole by the simple acts of forgiveness and acceptance. The funny thing is, I hadn't planned out any of this in advance. It just… happened. All I had to do was trust and let go.

My eyelids became heavy. I let go of my weakening grip on consciousness and drifted into a contented sleep I had not known since my childhood on the banks of the Hiwassee.

CHAPTER 29

The Fourth of July in Breckenridge, Colorado was an endearing little slice of Americana. The town was awash in red, white, and blue bunting. The Stars and Stripes flew from porches and businesses. Main Street was closed for a patriotic parade of cub scouts, fire trucks, classic cars, and marching bands. It was a Norman Rockwell painting come to life.

Miles and I were driven back to Breckenridge early to be reunited with our bikes and continue our journey. When we arrived at the bike shop, Wills was waiting for us. I was so touched by his kind gesture to see us off.

After loading our bags back onto our bikes, I turned to Wills to say goodbye. I didn't want to ruin the fragile spark of the previous day with imprecise words, and I didn't trust my skill at saying what my heart was feeling, so I just hugged him and shed a tear. I think he translated that better than anything I could've said.

"Bye Mom. Be careful."

"I will. Take care of that leg."

"O.K."

We rode away through the throng of gathering parade watchers along the closed street. We even got a few cheers of our own from the crowd. Soon we left civilization and entered the wilderness once more, and began the ascent to the second-highest point of the race, the 11,482 ft. Boreas Pass.

As we climbed, we were passed by a stream of mountain bike racers. The Firecracker 50 was part of the holiday festivities in Breck and had started after we left. The racers made quick work of Miles and me on our loaded steeds, and streaked uphill toward the pass. I knew several of the competitors from races past, many of whom shouted encouragement to me as they sped by.

"Gracie! Way to go, girl!"

"Tour Divide! Whoop-whoop!"

"Grace, take me to Mexico with you!"

Boreas Pass was the sixteenth crossing of the Continental Divide that I had made since leaving Banff. A railroad line once crossed here, spawning a tiny settlement that once boasted the highest-elevation post office in the country. Now, just a few ghostly structures remain, keeping silent watch over the forested patches of green below and the barren, purple peaks above.

The ride downhill from Boreas Pass was one with which I was well acquainted from racing the Firecracker 50 in years past. Known as The Gold Dust Trail, it was banked and smooth, and could be ridden fast without fear of sudden obstacles. I knew this. Miles didn't. I ripped down the trail and put distance between us.

Between the necessity of a companion for the Basin and my nervousness and excitement about Breckenridge, I hadn't put much thought into my trail marriage to Miles. What was supposed to be a two-day partnership for safety's sake had morphed into a six-day ball and chain.

It wasn't that Miles was a bad guy. He was a good man. But we had different riding styles, different goals, and different personalities. The incompatibilities I was willing to overlook at first began to gnaw at me in a familiar way.

My Cinderella betrothal to Prince Charming (a.k.a. Corey) began back in the fashionable quarters of upper-class Chattanooga, but got its official start just up the road in Vail. In 1982, I was introduced to the glittering lifestyle of the wealthy on a ski trip to the Colorado playground. I was mesmerized by the stylish ease that wealth provided and aware that I wouldn't get much of it with a home economics degree, so when Corey proposed to me on a ski slope, I accepted.

I knew it was coming. On the flight to Colorado, the engagement ring had been stashed in his mom's purse in a petite jewelry store bag. Corey's little sister was seated between me and his mother. Little Sis reached in the handbag and pulled out a ring box.

"What's this?" she cried.

Her mother snatched the box and quickly stuffed it back in her purse.

I pretended not to notice the commotion. I just looked out the window at the cottony clouds below and thought, "Oh, shit."

I felt a tug in my heart pulling me away, the differences between us palpable but undefined. It's a shame so much pressure is placed on us to make such life-changing decisions before we fully understand who we are, but life doesn't wait until we're ready. I hadn't yet developed the courage to trust my intuition. I did, however, understand the fear of destitution and societal pressure, so I succumbed to his proposal, not verbally, but through tears that he (and his hovering family) misinterpreted as tears of joy.

Old Money is used to getting what it wants. No Money gets taken along for the ride no matter what it wants. The years between our 1982 engagement and 1985 wedding played out according to that script...mostly. A grand social wedding was planned. I was told that I would wear Corey's mother's wedding dress. All the best families in town would be invited. All I could think of was how Rosemary would get monumentally drunk and embarrass everyone in attendance.

The engagement was stifling. At a time when I should've been discovering my identity, I abdicated in favor of security. Decisions were made for me. I became one of those sorority Stepford Wives, donning the straightjacket of conformity rather than face the fear and wonder of authenticity.

In a moment of clarity and courage, I broke up with Corey, and ran back to Chattanooga and Rosemary's weirdness. I was immediately excommunicated from the upper crust as damnation rained down from his parents. It has been said that hell has no fury like a woman scorned. Truly hellish is the wrath of a rich mother whose son has been dumped.

I found work as a seamstress and quickly learned how boring poverty can be. Curiously, I missed Corey as well. We began to date again, secretly, as his mother forbade him contact with me. When the cat finally escaped the bag, his parents were furious. As a condition of readmitting me to his graces, Corey's father demanded that I write a letter of apology to his mother.

Apologize for what?

Of course, I didn't have the courage to utter those words. I wimped out and wrote a simpering letter to her, apologizing for the crime of insulting the family's pride. I did get a concession of my own out of the bargain. Instead of being put on parade in a grand wedding, we had a small ceremony in their backyard.

Rosemary got drunk anyway.

I rode into the nearly abandoned town of Como. A few souls clung to this once thriving railroad town and it still had a working fire department. The firefighters kept a cooler of fresh ice water sitting on a folding chair outside for anyone who might need a refill. I stopped to fill my bottles and looked back up the road to see if Miles was coming. He was nowhere to be seen.

I rode on. A stealth divorce was not what I had in mind. It was cowardly, but I had a long history of not pushing back, preferring the easier task of running away. I did it with Rosemary, Corey, Corey's parents, and now Miles. I turned the pedals over and surged south, alternating between feelings of relief and shame.

I rolled into the little town of Hartsel. I stopped at a convenience store to get a Coke and some water. While I was resting, a northbound female rode up. We struck up a conversation. She asked if I was riding solo.

"Well, as of today, it would appear that I am," I responded.

She laughed. "Yeah, I was riding with a dude for a few days. He was getting on my nerves, so I ghosted him."

We were soul sisters, vagabonds and loners who preferred our own company so much we were willing to take the extra chances of encountering danger without a larger, stronger male to provide a measure of safety.

We visited for a long time. Sara was her name. We shared stories of the things we had seen and swapped intel of the things that lie ahead.

"How was the desert?" I asked.

"Hot," she said. "How were the mountains?"

"High," I said. We laughed.

"Did you see any bears?"

"Yeah, I saw one in Montana, but he was a pussy. You don't need to worry about the bears...unless you are wrapped in bacon."

I was enjoying myself so much, I lost track of time. We must have talked for over an hour, which was way longer than I had intended for minor rest stop. I knew I had stayed too long when Miles rode into the parking lot.

He dropped his bike and strode up to me, out of breath and visibly annoyed.

"You're going to have to time trial faster than that if you want to drop me," he said. I didn't have the heart to tell him that I had been sitting there for more than an hour, nor did I have the courage to say, "Yeah, about that partnership we have...it's over." All I did was say something coy about waiting for him, which I definitely wasn't.

Sara watched the scene unfold with a knowing, pitying smile. As she got up to continue her journey, she hugged me and whispered, "Ditch him as soon as you can."

It should've been the easiest thing in the world to do. This was my race and I had the right to ride it with or without company. And if I had confronted Miles with my wish, he would've been cool enough to shrug his shoulders, say okay, wish me well, and ride off on his own.

That's not what happened. Instead, I folded. Once, I was Grace the badass goddess who stood astride the Continental Divide, rode her bike a thousand miles through the wilderness, fought hordes of mosquitoes, slept on a bed of gravel, and stared down a Grizzly bear.

Now I was a humble bike wife, the always smiling sorority girl who waited for her man to tell her which direction to ride, a submissive junior partner in my own adventure. I hated the feeling and hated myself for being such a weenie.

Miles refueled and we rode off, together again. We turned our bikes into a headwind that made it nearly impossible to cover ground, but I wasn't sure if it was the wind or a reignited depression that made my legs feel so heavy.

CHAPTER 30

I woke up the next morning in my tent. A fast-moving, angry storm had driven us to seek shelter in a cow pasture the previous night. There had been no time to find a more suitable spot to pitch our tents, so we hastily poached a campsite, tossing cow patties out of the way as the growling wind whipped around us.

We packed up in a more leisurely way after this episode of lawbreaking than we did back at the sheep ranch. The only eyes that were nearby to judge us were those of the cows, and cows could not care less about anything. Once we started riding, we topped an unnamed pass and began a long, gorgeous descent into the quaint town of Salida.

Considering all the eye-popping scenery I had witnessed on this race, it would be high praise to call anything the *most* beautiful. Yet if any scene could distance itself from the pack, it would've been the sight of the "fourteeners" of the Collegiate Peaks in the Sawatch Range. This collection of massive 14,000-foot mountains rises like a purple crown striped with lingering snow, forming a postcard-perfect backdrop to the delicious green of the Arkansas River valley winding peacefully below. Yellow-leaved aspens framed each sublime scene.

Ho-hum. I didn't care. Another stupid mountain in this stupid race on this stupid bike. The twin disappointments of the end of my visit with Wills and my failed escape from Miles had left me emotionally depleted. I was ready for the race to be over, but still had nearly 1,000 miles to go.

Miles and I decided to cut the day short. I was not feeling the whole "ride-a-bike-across-the-country" thing, and as we looked at the map, we thought it might be best to "lay up," (a golf term used to describe a conservative shot up to the edge of a hazard, giving the golfer a better chance of clearing the hazard on the next shot, which aptly described our situation) because the hazard to which we were laying up was a doozy. Four gigantic mountain passes including the granddaddy of them all, Indiana Pass, awaited us over the next 150 miles. It promised to be the most strenuous section of the entire route.

We found two rooms at an inn in Poncha Springs. I went to my room to be alone. I hadn't realized how much seeing Wills had meant to me. Wills had been a carrot that pulled me from Canada to Colorado. Actually, he had been *the* carrot, the subconscious force which kept me going even as stronger, faster riders dropped out. Despite my many obstacles, I felt like nothing could stop me from seeing my son.

Now that Breckenridge was behind me, I lost desire. The Mexican border meant nothing to me, and I felt the Tour Divide slipping away from me. I called Kym to see if she could provide a swift kick in the ass.

"Kym, I need a carrot."

Kym collected her thoughts for a moment and began.

"Grace, Antelope Wells is your carrot. The end of the race. You have come so far, passed so many tests, but the biggest one remains, and that is 'will you finish?'"

"I *can* finish," I peeped.

"I know you *can* finish. Your physical strength is beyond question. Now you are in the realm of the mind. The will. I have seen your will before. It is an impressive thing to witness, unstoppable when you engage it."

"I seem to have lost my will."

"Yes, this is the darkest point of your journey. Recognize and accept that, but realize that this will pass. Did you hear me? This. Will. Pass. Once you clear this hurdle, you will sail to the border."

"How do I do that?"

"I don't know," she laughed, "How do you eat an elephant?"

CHAPTER 31

One bite at a time.

Miles and I sat down with a map to count our bites for the rest of the race. I thought it would make me feel better to have some clarity about how much more of this to expect. The outcome was disheartening. After thirty long days on the bike, we still had eleven more riding days to reach Antelope Wells, each with more than seventy miles to cover, and included three big days of more than ninety miles, and one monster 120-mile day in the New Mexico desert.

Miles and I saddled up and began the day. It might have lifted my mood to have an easy day pedaling alongside a tranquil river, but no, the Tour Divide was called a *mountain* bike race for a reason. A long and relentless climb up to Marshall Pass greeted us immediately. I became cranky. By the time we reached the little settlement of Sargents on the other side of the mountain ("Population few, Elevation high," the town sign read), I was full of venom and needed to spit. I snapped at Miles as he began his ritual of taking off gear in preparation for a long, leisurely rest break.

"You have thirty minutes. We don't have time for an hour-long break."

Miles looked at me curiously. I had never displayed irritation towards him before. He said okay and went about his business. I stewed with annoyance as I watched him continue his ritual. I steeled myself to ride off without him when thirty minutes had passed.

Thirty minutes later, he was on his bike and ready to go. We rode in silence for the rest of the day, climbing another big mountain to our second CD crossing and campsite for the night at Cochetopa Pass. Cochetopa is a Ute Indian word for "pass of the buffalo." We never saw any bison, but in the middle of the night, a pack of coyotes ran shrieking through the campsite, making my hair stand on end.

The next morning, Miles thanked me for pushing him the day before. We made eighty-four miles with two CD crossings even though neither one of us felt much like riding. I had to admit to myself it was a good thing to have Miles with me. I was so depressed after my climactic visit with Wills, I wanted to quit. Only my connection with Miles, however tenuous, and a feeling of obligation to him kept me going. In a weird and conflicted way, I was grateful for his presence.

But I wasn't going to tell him that. I was still going to leave his ass. Soon.

Maybe.

The day unfolded much like the previous day, with long, hot climbs along uninspiring, dusty forest service roads. The fatigue, physical and emotional, was beginning to mount as we summited the 10,000ft. Carnero Pass. We were sucking down water at an accelerated rate. By the time we reached the turnoff to the hamlet of La Garita, we were nearly empty. The fifteen miles of riding to our hotel in the town of Del Norte, coupled with the heat of the day, meant continuing without water was out of the question. We detoured off the route and headed east into La Garita find some water.

Until this point in the race, the parade of "things that might kill Grace" included hypothermia, a bike wreck, altitude sickness, landslides, drowning, falls from high cliffs, being hit by a car, lightning, bears, cougars, wolves, waterborne parasites, and exposure. For the rest of the race, dehydration would vault to the top of the catalog of concerns. Surface water and resupply towns, always conveniently spaced to the north, would become sparse as I plunged deeper into the desert. As a result, I wasn't about to screw around with my water supply. I was always monitoring it.

Miles and I split up to look for water in La Garita. The lone resident I saw was a man on an ATV riding circles in his yard as his dog ran behind him. I was tempted to ask the man for water, but hesitated. The scene reminded me of the oddball I met in Montana with the dog named Rocky who bit me, except this man had the vaguely sinister look of a drug dealer. I had neither the desire to get bitten again nor have a cap busted in me. (Getting shot was not on my list of TD dangers, so I did not prepare for that.)

As I was ruminating about drug dealers, dogs, and gunshot wounds, Miles rode up and broke my trance. He had found a working pump in a deserted campground. We hastily rode to the campground, refilled, and got out of town. I continued to daydream about a chance encounter turning into a crime. I wondered how many times on this journey I had been just a moment or decision away from becoming a victim of violence. As I created alternate scenarios from the past, a real and present paranoia rose up in me.

I was fully engulfed in this fantasy when I rode around a bend at the top of a hill and saw a real man standing along the trail in the valley below. A bike lay casually at his feet, so I surmised he was not one of the murderers or rapists who had been dancing in my head. On the other hand, I also acknowledged that a murderer or rapist would be brilliant to include a bike as a prop to get a gullible victim to let down her guard. I stopped at the top of the hill, watching the man through squinting, skeptical eyes as I talked myself out of the irrational foolishness which had overwhelmed logic.

I rode down the hill, wondering how long it would take for Miles to ride up if my horrific fantasies came to pass. I decided to ride up to the man to say hello. The killer waved, smiled, and called me by name. The murderer I had created in my mind turned out to be an old friend.

Bobby Smith was a mountain bike buddy and past TD finisher. He had driven from his home in Kansas to surprise me with a visit. I was so overwhelmed with gratitude and joy, I burst into tears and squeals of delight.

"What are you doing here?" I yelled.

"Just popped over to see my favorite southern belle, ma'am."

"Pssshh, southern belle. You came a long way to see a broken-down old broad."

"You, ma'am, are worth it...and you're not broken down."

As I hugged him and shouted in disbelief, Miles caught up. He shook Bobby's hand formally, without any warmth. The three of us rode into town together. I bent Bobby's ear telling him story after story. I could feel the positive energy returning with each crank of the pedal. Trail angels bear many kinds of gifts. Most give gifts of food. Some give shelter. My trail angel, Bobby, gave me something intangible, but the most valuable thing I could receive at exactly the right time. He gave me the gift of renewed spirit.

By the time we reached the outskirts of Del Norte, I felt whole again. The darkness that had shrouded my soul had lifted thanks to a well-placed trail angel. Kym was right. "This will pass," she had said. It had passed and I rejoiced.

The final mile of the day's journey included a crossing of yet another legendary American river, the Rio Grande. From this point, the river would travel some 1,800 miles and drop almost 8,000 ft. to make it to the Gulf of Mexico. Like the Rio Grande, I would leave the mountains of Colorado and cross the length of New Mexico. The difference was that once I got to the other end of New Mexico, I would stop, but the river would not. It would keep seeking until it found the sea though it did not know the way. This thought felt familiar. The Tour Divide in all its immensity would not quench my wanderlust any more than the Mexican border could satisfy the Rio Grande. Once the race was over, I would rest for a bit, then roll again. Where, I did not know. I would not reach my "Gulf of Mexico" until the warmth drained from my legs and the last breath left my lungs. As long as there was a path in front of me, I would keep following it, just like the river.

CHAPTER 32

I was glad my mental fog lifted before the next day. I would need all my faculties and emotional strength to face the giant of the Tour Divide, Indiana Pass. The pass soars nearly 12,000 ft. above sea level. While I was no longer concerned about altitude sickness, the sheer size of the climb was daunting. Twenty-three miles and 4,000 ft. of altitude change stood between me and the roof of this race.

I said my goodbyes to Bobby. He hugged me and said cryptically, "I'll be in touch." I wasn't sure what he meant, but as he said it, he cut a glance at Miles. The impending doom of my trail marriage was apparently the worst kept secret on the Tour Divide. Still, Miles and I rode into the mountains together.

It is said that mountains make their own weather. A sunny day in a valley can become a blizzard a few thousand feet up. Moisture laden fronts slam into the flanks of a mountain which squeezes rain, snow, or hail from the clouds as they rake across the summit. Lightning can strike. Frigid winds can cut through ill-prepared visitors. Freak summer storms can strand even backcountry experts, and wet plus cold is a recipe for hypothermia at any time of year.

We would play this game of chicken with Mother Nature over the next hundred miles, most of which would take us higher than 9,000 ft., and about half of that would climb over 10,000 ft. There was no way around it, the only thing to do was run the gauntlet and hope for fair weather.

The gauntlet seemed interminable. We climbed and climbed. I pushed the bike when I got tired of riding. The pain of the journey up to Indiana Pass was somewhat ameliorated by the wildflowers that littered either side of the trail. Columbine, Paintbrush, and Fireweed speckled the slopes in a riot of colors as snow-capped mountains formed a serene backdrop. Once again, I was surprised and awed by the beauty that thrives in this hard place.

Other than fatigue and the murder of a few thousand calories, Indiana was crossed without incident, and strangely without a sign to mark the highest point of the race. Only later did I remember the pass is not part of the Continental Divide, so it did not rate one of the familiar brown and yellow markers the park service erects at major passes.

The route kept us above 11,000 ft. for many miles, but the sun never failed us. I can't imagine how much harder Indiana Pass would have been if harsh weather had been thrown into the mix. After the high point of the pass, we gradually leaked about 3,000 ft. of altitude until it was time to climb again.

Miles was suffering mightily. I had to coax him up the paved road to La Manga Pass. The fatigue of the body eventually spreads to the brain, kicking off a cascade of anti-social behaviors. Miles became surly and snappish. I rode on ahead to allow him the space to curse in private.

It was hard riding, but I eventually came across a sign that sent me into a spasm of utter joy. The sign read "Welcome to New Mexico." The last state. I gleefully stopped and took a series of selfies with the sign. Miles rode up while I was in the middle of posing in peace-and-pout.

"Hey Miles, come and get a picture with the New Mexico sign!"

"No," he said, and kept on riding.

Twenty feet later, he stopped and turned around. "Oh, alright, I'll wish I had later."

On our last climb of the day up Brazos Ridge, the weather finally caught up to us. A fast-moving storm chased us into our tents. It was just as well. It had been a long day and Miles was toast. I hoped a good night's sleep would cure his crabbiness.

I got my answer first thing the next morning. While breaking camp, Miles asked if I had any more Gatorade in my bottle. I answered yes as kindly as I could.

"Gimmie some," he snapped. I stared laser beams through his skull as I handed over the bottle.

"I want a divorce," I said plainly to Corey. Thirteen years of being miscast as the dutiful southern housewife had taken every ounce of joy out of me. I finally reached my endpoint of being the second banana in my own life. It's not that Corey was abusive or neglectful. He was a good man. He provided for me honorably as a husband. Early in our marriage, he asked me to give him a budget for my needs. I was so unaccustomed to the habits of the wealthy, I misunderstood his request.

"You mean for groceries and gas?"

"No, for things you want, like shopping and lunches with girlfriends."

Here I was, the poor girl who made her own clothes, being given a discretionary income to buy clothing and jewelry just to impress the other idle trophy wives. At first, I felt like a lottery winner, but over time I began to resent feeling that I was a piece of property, not to mention the waste and shallow consumption that passed for living among the well-heeled.

In the months leading up to my declaration, I visited five attorneys. The first four gave me figurative pats on the head along with patronizing advice about treating depression. Those gray-headed throwbacks basically suggested that I go home, cook a nice meal for my man, and all would be right in the morning.

Jerks.

The fifth lawyer agreed to represent me. Once the attorney was on board, I went to confront Corey. When I told him of my intention, he was floored. He had not realized how unhappy I had become, but he agreed to find a lawyer to represent him. In another punch to the gut, he went to the same five attorneys I had visited, only to have each of them say that they could not represent him because they had already talked to me. I can only imagine the sense of betrayal and embarrassment he felt as he walked out of each office.

It was never my intent to hurt him, but I had to leave. I had to save myself or slowly turn into Rosemary.

Once again, I was faced with the choice to leave a man. I was reminded of an old Hall and Oates lyric, "*The strong give up and move on, the weak give up and stay.*" I had many moments of weakness in my life and more doubt than I cared to remember. My prolonged association with Miles was just the most recent example. The depression I thought was banished by Bobby Smith's visit was slowly creeping back in. This time, I diagnosed it quickly. This time, there would be no hesitation. This time, there would be no lawyers to consult. This time, I would be strong.

This time, I left him for good.

The route took us out of the high Rockies into a mesa-filled wonderland. Other than one more foray above 10,000 ft., the Tour Divide was on a downward trend that would take me to the border. It had already been established that I was a far better descender than Miles, so I laid on the gas to put time and distance between us.

I hadn't worked out how I was going to stay ahead. Slow as he was, Miles always caught up to me when I stopped. I preferred to ghost him, hoping to avoid an uncomfortable confrontation. The answer to my problem came in the form of another trail angel.

I rolled into the rundown village of Vallecitos. This town was founded in 1776 during the Spanish colonial period and looked like it hadn't seen much improvement since Thomas Jefferson authored the Declaration of Independence. By chance, I came upon a man and slowed down to say hi. He was a local pastor who served his down-and-out flock with what must have been the love of Jesus and the patience of Job.

"Grace, if you need a place to stay tonight, I have a B&B."

"Really?" I exclaimed.

"Well, it's really only one B," he laughed. "The breakfast part will be on your own."

I patted the Ludicrous Food Bag and explained that I brought breakfast with me. He took me to a ramshackle adobe house with a corrugated tin roof. All kinds of junk sat on the front porch, rusted barbeque grills, furniture, and building supplies. A bulletin board on the wall held papers announcing items for sale, lost pets, and business offerings. The building served as a community center, thrift store, and flophouse.

The inside was just as cluttered. Musty books were stacked atop mismatched tables. Furniture and unwanted appliances were shoved into every corner. A thick coat of dust on every item told me that things were seldom brought in and nothing ever left. There was a sad finality to it, a feeling that these items and this town would never experience happy usefulness again. On the other hand, I felt a sense of kinship with it all. Away from the pressure to perform, the discarded items and I were free to rest, unseen and unhassled by the world and its expectations.

Chapter 33

I was awakened the next morning by a text from Bobby Smith. He had been watching our dots since I left him in Del Norte and he had news.

Miles is ahead of you. If you meant to leave him, be careful not to catch up.

I was discombobulated by this turn of events. I thought Miles had a slim chance to reach Vallecitos, but I did not suspect that he would get ahead of me. I texted Bobby and thanked him profusely. If he hadn't messaged me, I would've put the hammer down on the incorrect assumption that I was still ahead…and run smack into him.

I hadn't put any planning into my trail divorce. I only had the hazy idea that I would ride him off my wheel and he would be unable to catch me. In reality, Miles had ridden through town as I had inadvertently hidden like a rat in these modest and unadvertised accommodations. Even rats get lucky breaks sometimes. As I considered the state of things, this turned out to be a better option than running. I would no longer have to look over my shoulder like a fugitive. I breathed a heavy sigh of relief, grateful to be able to relax and ride without anxiety.

I was free.

Surrounded by junk, I finalized the end of my trail marriage with a toast of Gatorade.

My fucking Gatorade.

I began my most leisurely day on the Tour Divide by leaving late and riding slow. I only had to ride some thirty miles to get to my next stopping point in Abiquiu. I lolled on the bike like I was riding a beach cruiser on a boardwalk, making lazy arcs back and forth across the road. I spent the morning in a state of mental rest, relishing my liberation and puttering along like

I had nowhere to go and all day to get there. I took some time to notice the landscape which had changed by almost imperceptible degrees, but was dramatically different from the north. Gone were the jagged peaks and rushing streams. In their place were mesas, and long, dry stretches of plains interrupted by intermittent remnants of long-dead volcanic peaks.

The midpoint of the day's short ride was a one-horse town with a famous calling card. It seems every state has that one hole-in-the-wall restaurant that is renowned across the entire state. The town of El Rito, New Mexico had the distinction of being the home of El Farolito, a little Mexican joint with a big reputation. The place even pulled out-of-state tourists to this nondescript, dilapidated village in an underwhelming corner of the southwest.

I made sure I rode slowly enough so I didn't miss the lunchtime opening. As I was entering the café, I decided to take a few selfies. A tourist arrived about the same time and drawled an offer to take my picture.

That accent.

I hadn't heard that in many months, but it was as familiar to me as the sound of rain. I pegged her for a Georgia native. Probably Augusta or Savannah.

She was from South Carolina.

Close enough.

A devoted foodie, she had made her pilgrimage to El Farolito at exactly the same time as me. We went in and had lunch together.

"Honey, what's a girl from Alabama doing out here on a bike?" she asked.

"I'm doing a race from Canada to Mexico."

"Lord have mercy, by yourself? Lord, that would scare me to death."

"Well, you gotta wanna," I said, falling back on my stock responses.

We talked as if we were cousins at a family reunion. It's a peculiar thing about southerners. We have a mystical connection to each other and our homeland, borne of the common culture of the Scots-Irish immigrants who settled in the south, the devastation and long-lasting aftermath of the Civil War, and the mocking scorn of the rest of the country. We speak a secret language of solidarity in the face of ridicule and kindness in a world of cynicism.

My newest trail angel paid for my lunch, then sprayed me with sunscreen, and gave me two frozen water bottles. She was what I would expect in a southern trail angel—generous to the point of mothering. I stuffed the water bottles in my jersey's back pockets to help with cooling on this sweltering day, and coasted a long, pleasant downhill to the hippie town of Abiquiu.

The mountains have always attracted the less traditional among us, the misfits who don't quite belong in the regular world of ambition and achievement. These non-conformists march to the beat of their own drummer and seek clarity only mountains can provide. I belong to this tribe, but while I find my purpose in the wild, open spaces of the Rockies or the Appalachians, I can also function in the everyday culture of America and can even pass for one of the squares when I need to.

Then there are those places that draw individuals who float even further out of the mainstream. Abiquiu is one of those places. It is reputed to be a center of universal energy (whatever that is) and as such, has drawn the spiritually adventurous to its vortexes for hundreds of years. In the 1700s, the place was so overrun with hippies—they called them witches back then—that the Spanish government sent soldiers to stamp out the rampant heresy. Abiquiu became so infamous, it was known as the Salem of the desert. Since then, it has attracted the full spectrum of religious practitioners, from Native Americans to Buddhists. A group of Muslims even built an impressive white mosque on a nearby hill.

The spiritual descendants of the Abiquiu witches were still there when I rode into town. I got a room at a bed and breakfast which doubled as a cleansing retreat where guests could purge themselves of all manner of negative vibes through meditation, massage, or other New Age rituals. All the female guests, ladies in their sixties and seventies, were garbed in the traditional hippie uniform—flowing skirts, paisley headscarves, turquoise jewelry, and Birkenstocks. Some of the Bernie Sanders-looking dudes even had on tie-dye t-shirts, for crying out loud. The stereotypes were so perfectly recreated, I would've sworn that they were all cast members from an *Austin Powers* movie still in costume. The sixties must've left a powerful impact on them to make the summer of love persist for fifty years.

It was all so groovy.

CHAPTER 34

The Tour Divide had only one start, but it had many beginnings. Abiquiu was the beginning of the end, and the beginning of the most perilous section of the whole race. The north, while more mountainous, was relatively more populated, which supported more towns and services for the racer who was tired, hungry, out of water, or had a broken bike. It was also cooler in the north, which helped keep MS at bay.

New Mexico would not be so hospitable. Long stretches of hot, dry, empty country would test my logistical expertise (which was non-existent) at riding great distances in the desert. With this in mind, I began to stock my bike like a Tuareg nomad outfitting his camel for a trip across the Sahara. The extra food and water weighed heavily on my bike and my legs as I began the last major climb of the race up Polvadera Mesa.

Polvadera was considered the hardest extended climb of the whole Tour Divide. Like Indiana Pass, it was a 4,000 ft. elevation gain to the top. It stretched for nearly thirty miles. To top off its superlatives, there would be no services over the entire eighty miles I had to cover to get to Cuba, New Mexico. No towns, no lodges, no convenience stores. If anything bad happened, I would face it utterly alone, miles and miles from help.

To get a jump on the sun, I left Abiquiu and the sleeping hippies at 4 a.m. It was an eerie feeling—being alone in the wilderness at night with only a narrow beam of light keeping me from being swallowed by infinite darkness. I had only covered ten miles as the approaching sun drew a pink line across the horizon. It would be a long, hot day.

I climbed throughout the morning as the benign sun turned oppressive. I tried to shield my face from the pounding by wearing a floppy brimmed visor under my helmet, but the Polvadera's white volcanic slickrock reflected the light into my eyes from below. I became inexplicably sleepy. At one point, I had a minor wreck. I fell off the bike into some soft dirt. As if shot by a tranquilizer dart, I fell instantly asleep.

I don't know how long I was out. To say the least, I was a little alarmed when I awoke. This was something that had never happened before. I didn't know if it was a measure of my cumulative exhaustion or if something else was happening.

Either way, the only thing to do was press on and get to Cuba. As I neared the paved road that would take me the last ten miles to town, it began to rain, then sleet. The road dropped steeply off the mesa to the valley below, rocketing me down the rain-slicked pavement on what would be the last big downhill of the race.

I forgot to take off my visor before I started my descent. That was stupid. The floppy brim did what floppy brims do. It flopped. Over my face. As if a steep, wet road wasn't enough of a challenge, I would be doing it blindfolded.

To slam on the brakes would have been suicidal. The wheels would have locked and I would have lost what little control I had; sliding, falling, and breaking things—mostly myself. I had to ride it out while braking ever so slightly until I came to a controlled stop. Controlling the bike didn't worry me, not being able to see where I was going was tremendously concerning.

I cocked my head to the side to see around the end of the visor. I only had a sliver of vision out of one eye, but it was enough to keep me between the lines. I fancied myself a one-eyed pirate, but then it occurred to me that only the world's most moronic pirate would put a patch over both eyes.

While I was slowing, a motorcycle rider passed me going the opposite direction. I was grateful he was going the other way. I didn't want to see him again and have him ask me if I was the idiot riding her bike downhill with a visor over her face.

After stopping safely and regaining my composure, I removed the visor and continued to the outskirts of Cuba and a roadside Subway restaurant. I went in to get some grub and inquire about the local motel rankings.

As the two sandwich artists were working on my two giant subs, I asked which was the best motel in town. They stopped with handfuls of pickles, looked at each other and snorted.

"You mean the least awful motel?" one of them offered. They laughed.

I ate one of the sandwiches and packed the other for later. I rode to the least awful motel and checked in. A time-worn old lady with deep creases in her face was working the front desk. Her sagging, folded skin betrayed a hard-lived life. As I was completing my registration, a striking man, tall, but not too tall, and wrapped in black leather, walked in carrying a motorcycle helmet. He looked at me in my cycling getup.

"Rain was cold," he said.

"Yeah," I replied.

He studied me silently for several seconds, as if trying to solve a riddle.

"Are you the lady who was riding down 126 from Polvadera?"

I sighed. "Yes."

"Were you wearing some kind of rain shield on your face?"

Oh boy, here we go. Do I make up some ridiculous lie about a new piece of rain gear or come clean?

I decided to tell him the truth. We both had a good laugh along with the lady behind the desk. The motorcyclist motioned to my bike which was dripping water on the lobby floor and spoke again.

"You need to put a motor on that bike."

"Nah," I replied. "That would be too easy."

CHAPTER 35

I stood naked in front of the little bathroom mirror of my room and gazed at the skeleton before me. A half-eaten sub sandwich rested in its wrapping paper on the corner of the bed. Despite eating everything I could get my hands on throughout the last few weeks, I was still losing weight. Worse still, my skin was a bony wad of distressed leather, a walking piece of beef jerky. Deep gouges segmented my lips. I ran my fingers across them and along weathered cheeks. I traced my jawline from ears toward my chin and stopped midway.

The grape-sized lump that I had noticed in Banff had grown almost into a golf ball. Swollen lymph nodes were no big deal to me. I experienced them anytime I got sick. The thing that alarmed me was that I had no other symptoms of infection. And it was so big.

I hope I don't have cancer.

I snorted at the thought and my eagerness to jump to the direst possibility. I finished my sandwich and went to bed. The night's dreams were panicked vignettes of me eating a rotten sandwich, which caused me to get cancer, then trying to find my bike so that I could ride to the hospital, only to find the bike had no wheels.

The next morning, I decided to stay in Cuba and get my lump looked at by a doctor. I went to the desk and the same wrinkled lady from the previous afternoon was still there.

"Do they ever let you go home?" I joked.

"Home's lonely," she said, "I would rather be here." There was a pitiful resignation in her voice, a cold realization that the best her life would offer was greeting strangers in a shabby motel in the middle of nowhere. I smiled weakly at her, not knowing what to say.

I asked her if I could find a doc-in-the-box in town. She affirmed that Cuba did indeed have a walk-in clinic and gave directions. She then offered to leave her post at the desk and take me there. I declined her offer and walked the mile to the clinic.

The clinic was an uninspiring block building along the main road. Weeds grew from cracks in the sidewalk. The receptionist inside processed my paperwork with undisguised boredom. As I watched her go through the motions of her tasks, joyless and unmotivated, I was reminded of the Thoreau quote, "Most men lead lives of quiet desperation." As I sat in the waiting room and continued to watch the receptionist, I pondered this uniquely human and all too common condition. How is it that life, which is marvelous, rare, and vanishingly short, is too long for so many? And, more personally, how close did I come to living a life of bottomless despair had I not escaped the role of the southern society lady?

I was called back to see the doctor. He was a youngish man, flabby and unkempt. He reflected the depressing vibe of his workplace. He examined me half-heartedly. He showed little concerned about my golf ball, satisfied to chalk it up to some minor infection. He diagnosed me with mild dehydration and prescribed an antibiotic and rest. He then shuffled me out the door, probably anxious to return the eye-glazing parade of nothingness on the internet. The prescription was called in to a pharmacy further down the street. When I exited the clinic, I was supposed to take a right to find the drugstore.

I went left, headed back to the motel. As I walked, annoyed by the wasted morning at the clinic, and perplexed by the depression that permeated the town, a beaten, rusted Lincoln Town Car that was at least twenty years old pulled up beside me.

"You want a ride?" came a voice from the car.

It was the creased lady from the motel. She had left her desk after all to take a five-minute drive to fetch me. Her hospitality was appreciated, but I sensed that she was more interested in slaking her own thirst for company. I didn't have any more appointments scheduled that day, so I climbed in. She drove us to the motel and parked in front of the lobby. We sat in her car and talked for nearly an hour.

At some point in the rambling conversation, I made the self-conscious remark that she probably thought I was the strangest person she had ever met. She chuckled.

"Grace, my parents were carnies in a two-bit circus. Raging alcoholics and drug addicts, the most time they spent on me was the night I was conceived. I was raised by the Bearded Lady and the other circus freaks. I got to watch how they were mocked and insulted night after night and it broke my heart."

"People can be so mean," I said.

"Yes, they can. Now, you would think that people like that would become bitter about their lot in life, hateful and angry. But somehow those people transformed the grief and shame of their disfigurement into love which they poured over me. I began to see myself as one of them, the child of circus freaks. I've never been able to figure out how such beauty can come from such ugly circumstances, but I have learned that status or appearance or occupation are pretty poor methods for judging a person. I've learned to accept life as it is and people as they are. When I saw you last night; dripping wet, cold, alone, and smiling from ear to ear, I thought you might be a freak like me."

I must have made a face at being called a freak. She hurried to recover.

"When I say 'freak,' I mean that as the highest compliment, as in a freak who lives outside the mainstream, a person who trades the comfort of conformity for the unpredictability of being real. My circus family was assigned the role of freak at birth and did the best they could with it. You chose it freely. That takes courage."

I didn't know what to say to all that, so I just said, "Wow."

She caught herself and became embarrassed. "I'm sorry that I have taken so much of your time when you should be resting, it's just so rare to be around someone who radiates joy."

"I radiate joy?" I didn't feel like I was radiating anything but days-old sweat and exhaustion.

"Yes. You love your life as it is and it shows. You asked me if you were the strangest person I have ever met. You are strange. Do you know how strange it is to meet someone who is exactly who they are supposed to be?"

As I got out of the car, I asked her name.

"Nancy," she replied.

"Nice talking to you, Nancy."

"It was nice talking to you, too, Grace. Your name suits you."

"Oh really? I always considered it too religious sounding for someone who is not religious."

"*Grace* has many meanings," she said. "My favorite is 'a divine influence which operates in us to inspire virtuous impulses and to impart strength to endure trial.'"

I smiled at her, closed the car door and walked to my room.

Impart strength to endure trial.

I liked that. I would have to remember those words as I entered the desert for my final trial.

CHAPTER 36

Five hundred miles separated Cuba from the Mexican border. More immediately, 120 miles stood between me and my next stop in Grants, New Mexico. It would be the biggest bite of this whole elephant, so I headed out well before dawn. As I passed through the lobby, I expected to see Nancy sitting there so I could tell her goodbye. She wasn't at the desk, so I stood there under the sterile hum of the room's fluorescent lights for several minutes, waiting to see if she would emerge from the back room. She didn't come out, so I left the artificial sun of the lobby and disappeared into the darkness of Cuba.

Cuba was established by Spanish colonists in 1769. Over the years, it grew into a wild west town so notorious, travelers were warned not to get caught overnight in Cuba. By the time I arrived on my bike in the summer of 2018, the town had spent all of its lawless energy and had settled into a benign senescence. I rode through the sleeping village alone, unconcerned about desperados lurking in the shadows.

So, too, the Rocky Mountains ran out of steam in Cuba, having completed their official course from the icy reaches of northern Canada to the waning green of the Sierra Nacimiento just south of town. Or maybe the Rockies stopped at the edge of the desert out of respect, a realization that their callow exuberance did not yet belong in the ancient, sanctified space that formed the cathedral of mesas and primordial volcanoes.

It's no wonder that so many religions were born in deserts, the desert is a religion waiting on a prophet. It seemed to contain all of the knowledge of the universe in its stillness. It invites humanity to commune with it in solitude, but is impervious to humanity's grasp. It is the province of God, the forgetting Eden of coyotes and serpents.

As I rode, a feeling of reverence overcame me. Like some soaring gothic church in Europe, the desert wills its silence upon the visitor. The dirt and miles turned beneath my tires and I drifted into a state of semi-consciousness; unthinking, unknowing. Just being. The hippies back in Abiquiu would have been so proud.

My spontaneous meditation was broken by the sight of two human silhouettes walking on the road far ahead of me. As I neared their position, I looked at my computer and panicked.

Shit, I'm off the route.

I must have missed a turn in my ecstasy, but I didn't remember passing a junction. I rode up to the two people to ask directions. They were Native American men dressed in flannel shirts, blue jeans, and work boots. I assumed they were headed to a job site, though we didn't seem to be near any kind of business.

"Hey guys, good morning!" I chirped.

"Hello, lady," one of them replied.

"You guys headed to work?"

They laughed. "No, we're headed home from the bar."

I looked around. There wasn't a bar within miles, so they must have been walking a long time.

"Yeah, we were just chillin' with some beers, you know, when this man walks up and says we have to go."

The other chimed in, "Yeah, we weren't doin' nothin', man. And he just kicked us out."

"That's awful," I said in solidarity. "Hey, I was wondering if you knew where..."

"We were just mindin' our own business, man, havin' a couple of beers. Threw us out for nothin'."

It finally dawned on me that the two were still drunk. I pressed on anyway.

"Yeah, that stinks. So, I'm trying to get to Cabezon Community Reservoir. My computer shows I am on the wrong road. Do you know where it is?" I doubted their answer even before they spoke.

"Oh yeah, you're on the right road. Just keep goin' and turn right at the next junction."

I thanked the men and rode on. They may have been sure about my direction in their inebriated hubris, but my sober GPS was not. It continued to flash "OFF ROUTE" at me. I cursed myself for taking the word of two drunks and turned back.

"Hey fellas, my GPS is still telling me I'm off the route. Are you sure it's this way?"

"Yeah, yeah. Just keep goin', you'll see it."

Their certainty convinced me, if only barely. I turned around and rode even farther than I did the first time. Still nothing on the GPS. I knew I had to turn around but I was too embarrassed to face the guys again. After weighing my options, I realized that I had no choice but to go back a third time.

As I approached the men, I sped up. I could see the incredulous looks on their faces as I passed them without making eye contact or speaking. I rode back up the road for miles until it became clear that there was no turn I missed. The men were telling the truth, which meant that I would have to face them one more time.

I rode up to them with the humility of a penitent. They eyed me with the kind of suspicion reserved for observing a lunatic.

"I'm so sorry. I'm doing this big race from Canada to Mexico and I have to follow the route without deviation. My GPS must have crapped out on me. You say it's up this way?"

They relented a little and decided that they had better give the crazy blonde chick some more detailed instructions. "Yeah, yeah. You see that mesa ahead? Ride up through the canyon. When you get to the dead end at the top, go right."

The men reminded me a little of Rosemary. She was probably more functional drunk than sober, too. I thanked them and apologized profusely for my rudeness. I was glad I would never have to see them again and relive my embarrassment.

Sure enough, as I topped the canyon, the road came to a "T." I went right just like the guys told me. Almost instantly, the GPS reset and showed that I was indeed on the right route. The coincidence was creepy. Maybe the desert, which seemed both alive and dead at the same time, was truly a supernatural living entity and had given me a test in trust. If so, I failed miserably three times before accepting help.

I returned to the otherworldly scenery. Volcanic stumps poked out of the plain like fingers pushing against the underside of a bedsheet. The unnatural quiet persisted. Turning the pedals at a constant cadence became rhythmic and meditative and I once again fell into something like hypnosis. The usual parade of random thoughts drained from my mind's movie screen and I dissolved into the nothingness.

A truck passed me from behind and snapped me out of my trance. In the bed of the truck were the two drunks, waving and smiling. One of them shouted to me, "Ay, you are on the wrong road! Go back!" The two of them laughed uproariously through the dust kicked up by the speeding truck. I wagged a disapproving finger at them and laughed. I certainly deserved the ridicule. Just to be sure, I looked down at the GPS. I was on course.

The only civilization encountered on the day's ride was at a little outpost called Chaco Trade. It was nothing more than a drab little convenience store, an artificial oasis in a sea of sand and rock, but at that moment, it was the most beautiful place on earth. Air conditioning, cold drinks, and food waited inside for me. I didn't want anything else. Two stray dogs sauntered over to me with their tails wagging.

"Hello, John. Hello, Mikey."

My two drunk buddies were sitting out front with their backs against the wall. They immediately started in on me.

"Ay, lady, you're here! You sure you're on the right road?"

"Yeah," the other chimed in, "I think you missed a turn!"

We laughed. "What are you guys doing?"

"Ah, we're just chillin', waitin' for a ride."

I walked in the store. The manager met me near the door and spoke.

"Did those two bother you?"

"No, I met them on the road at Mesa San Luis. They're good guys."

The manager looked incredulous and corrected me, "They are bums. Always here begging for money."

I couldn't believe it. "Those two? They were so nice to me."

"Yeah, well, you don't look like you have anything, so they left you alone," he said.

I was just about to defend their honor (and mine) when a truck pulled into the lot and a man got out. One of my drunk buddies walked over to him, clearly asking for money. The manager saw this too and leapt out the door. He rousted the drunks off his property. My friends shuffled away like two scolded dogs.

CHAPTER 37

The town of Grants was a classic American boomtown with several industries enriching, then bankrupting, the city. It began its life in the 1880s as a railroad town. Over the next century, logging, farming (*carrot capital of the USA!*), uranium mining (*uranium capital of the world!*) and tourism have all had a hand in keeping the town from drying into a tumbleweed-infested ghost town.

The most famous of these was the fabled Route 66 which ran through the town. "The Mother Road" etched its way into the fabric of 20th century American culture and is celebrated in books and songs. The highway, which stretched some 2,400 miles (or about 300 less than the TD) from Chicago to Santa Monica, captured the spirit of expansive, newly mobile America, as thousands poured from the dust bowl westward to the promised land of California.

The road, along with its charming Art Deco gas stations and teepee-themed motels, has since been buried by the efficient, yet soulless, Interstate 40. The interstate system killed many towns that once thrived along Route 66, but Grants managed to hang on; diminished, yet surviving.

After riding for eleven hours, I completed my 120-mile journey to Grants in mid-afternoon. Route 66 still held the imagination of the town decades after its heyday with signs and businesses named after the road.

Despite my navigational errors, the big mileage day was one of the easier ones of the Tour. It's misleading to say that riding 120 miles on a bike even remotely resembles anything close to easy—it doesn't. A bike ride of that length takes every watt of energy out of a body, leaving a bone-deep exhaustion in its wake. However, the combination of smooth roads, moderate temperatures and an ever-so-slight tailwind helped tremendously. I was lucky. A desert scorcher or a headwind could've lit up my MS and things could've spun out of control. Maybe I passed the desert's test after all and it rewarded me.

My accommodations for the night were at a Motel 6. This downscale chain wouldn't make anybody's five-star list, but five-star comfort is a low bar when you're dog tired. A bed, shower, and air conditioning were the only things in the world I wanted, and would have felt no better at the Ritz Carlton.

A little drug store next to the motel advertised a sale on beer. "A beer would taste divine right now," I thought, so I went in to get one. They didn't have any regular size cans in singles, only a big 16-ounce monster. I bought one and took it back to my room. The thought of a beer exceeded the experience. Even my taste buds were tired. After a few sips, I abandoned the project and went to sleep instead.

It was probably a good thing that I didn't finish the mammoth beer. In my dehydrated and malnourished state, a single 16 oz. can would have probably had the equivalent impact as a two-day bender. Riding hungover was the least appealing thing I could think of.

The long stretch of 260 miles from Grants to Silver City would take three days. During that time, I would only encounter one restocking opportunity in a little village called Pie Town. So, one more time, I stuffed the Ludicrous Food Bag to the breaking point. This time, I bought those awful performance bars that have the consistency and taste of compressed earth. I made this choice based on the geekiest of reasons—the performance bars had the most calories for the least amount of weight. Also, because they were made from chemicals not found naturally on this planet, they would not melt in the desert heat. So, while I would have rather had something awesome like Snickers or Three Musketeers, I put on my big girl pants and purchased with maturity. I mostly stuck with "chocolate" flavor; not because it tasted anything like a real chocolate bar, but because it was the least likely to make me gag before I got it all down.

The day's ninety-mile ride to Pie Town was another uneventful stretch of gravel road. The only interest on the route was a few miles along the western edge of El Malpais National Monument. Malpais literally means *badlands* in Spanish. As recently as 1,000 years ago, small volcanoes vomited ropy black basalt here. Navajo legends still speak of the "fire rock" that burned the land. The rock no longer burned, but formed an uninviting landscape that still looked charred centuries later.

Pie Town was created by an enterprising young man looking to create a destiny for himself. He owned a service station when it was announced that Route 60 would be designated an official U.S. transcontinental route, like Route 66, but on a more modest scale. The man started offering homemade pies to travelers and erected signs along the road to advertise them. A small town grew up around the station. The town had no history or natural feature from which to draw a name, so the locals began to call it Pie Town. The name became official when the Postal Service gave Pie Town a post office and zip code.

Pie Town's pies were still famous. Many moons ago, when I started this race back in Canada, the organizers gave each racer a token, a bicycle stem cap, that could be exchanged for a free slice of pie at the Pie-O-Neer Café. I had carried the stem cap like a talisman for weeks. Sometimes, when I was low on inspiration, I would look at it and think how exciting it would be to trade it in when I made it all the way to Pie Town. *If* I made it to Pie Town. It was one of the head games I played with myself to keep going.

A few miles out of town, with my rendezvous with a free piece of pie all but assured, a disturbing thought barged its way into my brain.

What day is it?
Sunday, I think.
Oh no.

A funny thing happens when you don't have appointments to keep. The names of the days take on less importance until finally, you lose track of what day it is. Every few days I would make an effort to catch back up, but within a day or so I would forget again. It really didn't matter. Every business I needed was open seven days a week.

Except one. The Pie-O-Neer Café.

Now, I don't begrudge anyone for taking a day off. The hard-working folks at the Pie-O-Neer surely deserved to close at least once a week, and Sunday is a very common day to close.

But, dang, of all the luck. Out of the seven days of the week that I could have possibly arrived, it had to be this day. I reminded myself never to play Russian Roulette.

I decided to ride by the café just in case they had summer hours or something.

They were open!

I dug the stem cap out of the corner of a bag where it had made a home since my first day. Every item I packed had been used except this one. Now was its turn. I triumphantly presented the cap and got a slice of apple pie a la mode in exchange. I stared at the plate in front of me.

Long way to ride for a piece of pie.

Indeed it was. And worth every mile. I dug into the pie and savored every bite.

CHAPTER 38

The trail magic which started on the first day of the race continued. I checked into a little bed and breakfast in Pie Town. A man named Jerry, who managed an RV park next door, saw me ride in and came over to say hi. By this time, I was used to dot-watching strangers knowing my name.

"Hi Grace, I'm Jerry. Welcome to Pie Town. Great ride you're having."

"Thank you, Jerry. I have enjoyed it, but I think I'm ready to be done now."

He smiled. "I can imagine. You've come a long way. Let me wash your bike while you rest."

I handed the bike to him with thanks and limped toward my room. The toe that had been complaining since Montana was now screaming in pain. Jerry noticed.

"What's wrong with your foot?" he asked.

I told him about offending toe and he stopped fiddling with the bike.

"Let's take care of that first and then I'll get back to your bike. In addition to being a top-notch trailer park manager and bike washer, I'm also a first-class EMT," he said with a wink and a mischievous smirk.

Jerry doctored my toe expertly, cleaning and bandaging it with the skill of a first-class EMT. I asked him if he took Blue Cross.

"Naw, I usually only take cash, but this one is on the house," he said, laughing.

He disappeared out the door to return to the bike while I napped on my bed. When I woke up, it was almost bedtime, so I obliged and went back to sleep.

The next two days would be the final big test of the TD. The Gila National Forest had the potential to throw everything but the kitchen sink at me. Cold, heat, rain, wind, lightning, terrain, wild animals, and dehydration all lurked in the crevices of the future. It would take 185 miles of hard riding to discover which of these, if any, would pay me a visit.

My newly adopted schedule of pre-dawn starts was becoming habit. The desert was unsympathetic to the preferences of a lady of leisure, so it was up to me to adapt to its unnegotiable climate. I rode out in the coolness of night, wishing I could somehow bank it to spend in the noonday heat. My plan was to ride nearly one-hundred miles and camp at a forest service work center that had an accessible water source.

As I pedaled, the sun rose like a promise over the Plains of San Agustin, home of the largest radio telescope in the world, called descriptively yet uncreatively the Very Large Array. The pan flat valley was once the bottom of a Pleistocene lake fifty miles wide, teeming with life. Now, its lifespan had come full circle. If the sea represents the genesis of life, the desert is the place where life returns to the repose of eternity. The rising sun holds possibility, though, even in a place as seemingly sterile as this. A new day, and all the days to follow it, would bring change to the earth, the continuation of the circle. As I turned the pedals, I wondered if this place would ever be resurrected into a living lake again.

For now, the desert rests. It holds its breath while humanity scurries. In our young country, people work like bees in a hive. From coast to coast, ambition infuses the land with kinetic energy and bends it to the task of creating the restless dreams of man. The New Mexican desert will have none of this. It sits silent and dignified as people go about their ant-like business, content to pause and be, as humanity puffs itself up with fevered fantasies of immortality.

The Very Large Array was built in San Agustin because it is the very antithesis of noisy, grasping civilization. It is largely devoid of earthly radio waves that pollute the interstellar signal, allowing those who can be still to listen to the music of the heavens.

Be still and listen.

I listened, but the still part required a Jedi mind trick. One doesn't usually associate riding a bike with stillness, but by separating the body into two halves and concentrating on the upper half, a kind of stillness can be achieved. While the lower body worked rhythmically, I fixed my attention on maintaining a motionless top half. The result was a kind of meditative state that helped me float down the dusty road.

My meditation was so effective I remained energetic throughout the day. I had expected to be exhausted by the time I rode a hundred miles, but when I reached the work center, I didn't want to stop.

I kept going.

The miles disappeared under my tires. My odometer read 110 miles. Then 115. I reached 124 miles, beating my previous record of 120 just two days ago. I wanted to continue. I wanted to see just how far this machine that I had been tuning for 2,500 miles would take me, but ominous black clouds were rising quickly to the west. I set up my tent and entered it just as the bottom dropped out of the swollen clouds. My body was still cooking from the ride, so I stripped naked and lay on top of my sleeping bag. I woke up hours later shivering cold in the dark. Mother Nature had decided to throw one last rager at me. I crawled into my bag and listened in fear and wonder as rain, wind, and thunder lashed my tent for most of the night.

CHAPTER 39

I awakened the next morning exhausted. The big effort of the day before, along with the apocalyptic storm that kept me up most of the night, had drained me. Apparently, the machine wasn't all I had cracked it up to be. In reality it was a used, fifty-seven-year-old engine with an expired warranty and a whole lot of miles on it.

Remaining in the tent for the day wasn't an option. My food and water would not last another day. I had to press on sixty hard miles to Silver City.

The Gila Wilderness is spoken of in hushed tones among Tour Divide riders. It is not the tallest, or the longest, or even the hottest stretch of trail, but it is the most relentless. An interminable series of maddeningly steep uphills and downhills drain any remaining reservoirs of arrogance a rider may have. It is a rollercoaster in slow motion, a repetitive grind of too-short descents followed immediately by too-long climbs. Adding to the difficulty, the wide gravel road became a tiny ribbon of singletrack. The trail was encroached upon by tire-poking cacti. Ponderosa pine and juniper blanketed the steep hills, reducing my field of vision and giving me a slight feeling that I had been transported back home to the Appalachians.

Riding this beast required focus. Focus required energy. My tank was nearly dry.

Fatigue is the mother of mistakes, and my extreme weariness almost caused the biggest mistake of the race. The slopes were too steep to ride up, so I developed a rhythm of coasting downhill and then dismounting right before the bike stalled on the uphill. I would swing my right foot over the saddle and onto the ground while the left foot stayed on the pedal, then step off with the left and start walking. Over and over I repeated this move. Each time the swinging right leg got heavier and heavier.

The inevitable happened, and as Murphy's Law would have it, it happened at exactly the worst moment. As I was starting my dismount at the bottom of one of the hills, I heard an unmistakable rattling sound. I was mid leg swing when my eye caught the moving rattle attached to a large coiled snake. My calf caught the saddle, throwing me hopelessly off balance and inexorably toward the snake.

For the next few moments, my future—indeed my life—was completely out of my hands. A simple act of clumsiness had transferred my life's trajectory to a single decision by an angry snake.

The rattlesnake, bless his heart, weighed the possible outcomes of the impending collision and decided discretion was the better part of valor. He slunk away a millisecond before impact, the wise old soul. He likely would've been injured by the falling human, and even if he had managed to kill me with a poisoned bite, what could he have done with one hundred pounds of beef jerky decades past its sell-by date? Snakes don't chew, venom is too precious to waste on a vanity project, and foolish animals don't last long in the desert. This dude was no fool.

I, on the other hand, felt like the biggest fool in New Mexico. I had allowed fatigue and impatience to override good sense and caution. My impertinence left me sprawled across the trail with my face mere inches from the threatening spikes of a cactus.

Thankfully, I remained unpunctured by either cactus or snake. I picked myself up, shaken but unharmed, and moved on. The desert doesn't always give second chances. I considered myself lucky to have been the recipient of one. I exited the wilderness onto the relative safety of a paved road. The Gila had battered me, exhausted me, and damn near killed me. I cried tears brewed from a mystifying emotional recipe of fear, exhaustion, relief, and one last ingredient. Finishing the Gila meant that my ride was nearly over.

Near the town of Pinos Altos, I crossed the continental divide for the thirtieth time since leaving Banff. Since leaving Pie Town, I had crossed nine times, but all lacked the grandeur of crossing the snow-covered passes in the north. My crossings over the past two days were over nameless, impotent ridges.

As I started my long, therapeutic descent into Silver City, my cell phone regained service and blew up with texts of congratulations from dot watchers all over the country. I guess they figured once a rider made Silver City, finishing the last 124 miles was a given. The phone also pinged to let me know that I had a voicemail. I pulled over to the shoulder to listen. It was a man I had never met with a strange invitation.

"Hey Grace, this is Moose in Silver City. A little birdie told me you are riding the Tour Divide. I've been watching your dot and had planned on giving you a big welcome, but some of us are going out on a bike ride right now. I have rolled a big fatty and left it on my windowsill for you. Get started with that and let's party when I get back."

Party? Fatty? Apparently, Moose was under the impression that I was a twenty-something waif who could ride all day and smoke marijuana all night. My idea of a party was a warm shower and a clean bed. And air conditioning. No illicit substance could transport me to the realms of ecstasy like a blast of freon-chilled air from a humming window unit in a cheap motel.

I didn't respond to Moose. I would've had to tell him that I was less than a decade from Social Security and my partying days were long past. I decided to let the untouched joint on the window be my answer to his thoughtful invitation.

I decided to stay two nights in Silver City. I was still tired from my ordeal in the Gila and the logistics of the final push to the border would demand another pre-dawn start. I spent most of the day resting in my air-conditioned nirvana, but I had one piece of business that required action. My blinking tail light had stopped working. Since I would be riding in the dark on a road used by cars, a light was mandatory. Thankfully, the town was big enough to have a local bike shop.

I didn't feel like riding the bike or even walking to the bike shop. I discovered that Silver City had a city bus that made a stop near the store, so I boarded the bus for the quick, one-mile trip.

It wasn't quick, and it wasn't a mile. I didn't bother looking at the bus route, which definitely did not go straight to the store like I had assumed it would. With every stop, more locals piled in, greeting the other passengers with easy familiarity. After thirty minutes, I began to feel like I had crashed a party. The other passengers all knew one another, laughing and talking like classmates at a high school reunion.

Meanwhile, I was getting car sick. I hadn't been in a vehicle for this long in weeks and the unfamiliar motion became unsettling. After forty-five minutes of riding through Silver City and getting caught up on all the local gossip, the bus stopped at my destination. I staggered off the bus and threw up on the sidewalk. I looked up at the bus. The guttural sound of someone vomiting had captured the attention of the passengers and momentarily halted the conversation. They were all looking at me the way rubberneckers ogle a car crash on the highway, with a mixture of fascination and revulsion. I wiped my mouth with the back of my hand and retreated quickly to the bike shop.

After purchasing the bike light, I decided not to shame myself with another bus ride, so I walked back to the motel. I still made the trip in less time than it took me to get there. After a quick resupply at a nearby convenience store, I returned to my air-conditioned palace so I could get to sleep early.

Butterflies prevented me from an easy sleep. I was excited for tomorrow.

The last day. Hopefully.

CHAPTER 40

I can. I will. I am.

I had repeated that phrase every morning since adopting it back at Holland Lake in Montana. I said it one last time at the Quality Inn in Silver City, New Mexico at 3 a.m., once I was dressed and ready to go. I took a selfie in the full-length mirror. My sweet bike, the trusted steed that had carried me flawlessly for 2,600 miles, was in the picture. I put on my puffy hoodie because it was a brisk forty degrees outside. Attached to my helmet was an outrageous snap-on brim that I bought the day before at the bike shop. It made me look like a grandma going outside to work in her garden.

Silver City sat at the threshold of the mountains to the north and the great Chihuahuan Desert, the biggest desert in North America, to the south. It is also the highest. Though it felt like I had lost thousands of feet from the big peaks of Colorado and was nearing sea-level, Silver City was still perched at 6,000 ft. (more than 700 ft. higher than the mile-high city of Denver).

The 124-mile ride to the border would contain nearly one hundred miles of gently sloping downhill, or pancake flat, riding. If all went well, it would be a fast ride. Fast would be good. Trees don't grow tall where water is scarce. No trees, no shade... except for that produced by my ridiculously large brim.

In addition to my desire to finish quickly and get out of the sun for good, I had another reason for wanting to end this day. There was a danger present in the final fifty miles of the course, one that I hadn't encountered yet. My guide map said it best, so I will quote its warning. *"Due to drug trafficking and the flow of undocumented migrants, it is advised to use this route only during the day. You could encounter drug traffickers, the Border Patrol, 'minutemen' (unofficial militia groups), Mexican coyotes (traffick-*

ing humans over the border) undocumented migrants, and other tourists. If you do camp, do so well off the highway."

Holy cow, I'm going to take a bike ride in the middle of a war zone.

Of all the dangers I had either faced or avoided, it seemed that the most lethal one waited at the very end of the race. I had one card to play; ride like hell and don't let the sun go down before I get to the border. I sped out of Silver City. My new tail light burned a red streak through the blackness.

Chapter 41

Hello, John. Hello, Mikey.

I spoke these words along the Tour Divide anytime I saw two animals standing together. It was a small ritual which never failed to provide a little spark of motivation and nostalgia.

Shortly after my divorce, I had to take a job. I couldn't find any work as a seamstress, so I found a gig as a clerk in an outdoor equipment store. It was monotonous and stultifying to spend hours in a retail cage, but I had made my financial bed and it was time to lie in it.

Business was slow. It was always slow. Camping and backpacking were not popular pastimes in the sticky humidity of Alabama, so I spent hours just looking out the large plate glass window across the drab parking lot. Landscaping trees softened the unnatural edges of the L-shaped shopping plaza. I daydreamed about climbing the trees. I didn't realize it then, but it was the darkest time in my life, a crisis of identity caused by a yet unidentified need to be outside. I was lost in my own psychological wilderness, trying to get home to the actual wilderness.

My deliverer came in a most unusual form. One day a shaggy-headed man wearing unfashionable dad glasses and that uniform of the suburb, the polo shirt & khakis combo, came into the store. Like a heat-seeking missile, he came straight to me without looking at the displays of tents or boots.

"What's your name?" he asked.

"Sybil," I said without missing a beat, hoping he would pick up on the reference to the Sally Field movie about a woman with multiple personalities. He did.

"Well, this is going to be fun," he said. "All the people I know only have one personality, and most of them are dull." He smiled a goofy grin and chatted me up for a while and then asked me a question that would come to define my life for decades. "Hey, have you ever gone mountain biking?"

That's when my life started over. John took me mountain biking for the first time. I was terrible; running into trees, falling over, and stopping in fear before even the slightest obstacle. John did his best to teach me how to ride, but teaching was outside his sphere of talents. He was a bright man, yet he was unable to articulate the concepts of bike handling, relying on hand signals and sound effects to get his points across.

"Gracie, you have to *brrrrrrrr* over these rocks," he said, pantomiming riding over a patch of rocks. I was never able to translate *brrrrrrr* into a lesson I could use. It became clear he had to bring in reinforcements.

John introduced me to Mike, the yin to his yang. John was an engineer by trade, but he didn't fit the engineering stereotype of unsociable awkwardness and precision. He was freewheeling and unstructured, just the opposite of the pocket-protector image most associated with engineers.

Mike was just the opposite. Detail-oriented and adept at teaching, Mike was nevertheless a ne'er-do-well, a nomad who made his way through life one short-term job at a time. Depression stalked Mike and weighed down his spirit. He was deep and brooding, the kind of person who always looked like they were on the verge of either a breakthrough or a breakdown.

Mike taught me the fundamentals of trail riding; how to enter and exit turns, how to scout obstacles on the fly and identify the best line, how to distribute my weight over the bike to maximize traction. He taught me that a mountain bike was like a dance partner and that a good trail ride should look faintly like the jitterbug.

I got better. I applied the lessons learned and made progress, but the mechanics of mountain biking remained, well...

mechanical. My riding style was not natural. There was no flow. Then one day an angel appeared to give me a final lesson.

Her name was, in fact, Angel. The child of sixties hippies, with a brother named Lucifer, Angel was one of those rare creatures whose talent and effortless charm attracted everyone. She seemed to exist on a higher plane than the rest of us dirt-eating schmucks. She also had a gift for riding a mountain bike. I think she might have been an actual angel.

The four of us rode together and became a pack. I usually followed Angel so I wouldn't hold her up on the narrow trail. She had a fluidity that defied explanation. I couldn't break down her style into pieces that I could mimic and incorporate into my own. Hers was an art form, inaccessible to a philistine like me.

The missing piece revealed itself one day while I was following Angel through a tricky section of trail. She was dancing with the bike as usual. I watched her intricate ballet of balance and thrust as the bike pulsed beneath her.

Momentum. That was what I had been missing. It wasn't that Angel had been analyzing the trail and making dozens of complex decisions beforehand, she was just letting the bike roll and then reacting to the input. Where I had been trying to control all aspects of a ride, Angel let the bike make the decisions and then she made subtle corrections when needed. While I was combating the trail, she was communing with it.

It was an epiphany. It was also counterintuitive for a Type A personality. Increasing momentum meant more speed, which increased the chances of crashing. It also meant trusting a brainless machine, and relinquishing some of the control I had been holding like a miser.

"Gracie," John said, "That's what I was trying to tell you when I said you have to *brrrrrrr*. What I meant was that you have to be *brrrrrrrave*. Brave enough to let go."

Bravery didn't come magically. It was a choice, but it was also a process. I started entering races and improving dramatically. At forty-years-old, it was too late to think about pursuing a career as a professional racer, but it became my profession nonetheless. I eventually became a mountain bike teacher myself and a professional racer, in a sense, when a drug company involved in MS treatment invited me to join their racing team.

Ten years after our first meeting, John was visiting me from his home in New Mexico. I noticed a slight slurring in his speech. I mentioned it to him.

"I haven't noticed that, but I have been having trouble swallowing, lately," he said.

Within a few weeks, he was diagnosed with ALS, Lou Gehrig's Disease. Three years later, he was dead.

Two weeks after John's funeral, Mike decided that he was tired of playing the bad hand that he had been dealt and took his own life.

CHAPTER 42

Let go.
I didn't want to. Letting go was not in my vocabulary. I held on for dear life because, to me, control was life itself. I took control of my MS diagnosis and, with Rosemary's wisdom, defined it, rather than letting it define me. I was proud of the control I was able to exert. I was proud of the willpower I swung like a sledgehammer against victimhood and disintegration. It kept me from rusting indecision and propelled me to find my purpose. My life's motto, *find a way,* is a declaration of my belief in control, a promise to punch negative occurrence in the mouth with relentless action.

But even a healthy sense of responsibility can become corrupt in the gilded mansions of the ego. When we become obsessive Ahab, everything looks like a white whale to be tracked and slayed. I am guilty of that as well. I was guilty of ham-handed efforts to control my fragile self-image by shunning my sweet, eccentric mother. I was guilty of marrying unwisely because I thought that marriage was an acceptable means of controlling financial security. I was guilty of pushing away my son when I could no longer manage him. I was guilty of seeing the Tour Divide as a foe that, once conquered, would validate my iron-fisted philosophy.

Real control allowed me to harness my life. The illusion of total control that I fed so extravagantly made a mess of things. Had the deaths of John and Mike not happened so close together, I might have had more time to process each, but the one-two punch of the loss of both my friends was overwhelming. The pain was so suffocating, it made me feel like I was losing control. So, I suppressed the pain and took a pass on the lesson that mortality tried to teach. Instead, I threw myself into riding. Harder, faster, longer, angrier. Anything to distract myself and avoid the truth.

John and Mike taught me how to choose. They also introduced me to the idea of the limits of choice, and the beauty of relinquishing control and letting momentum take over. This understanding eluded me on a bike for a long time. It eluded me in life even longer. I stopped momentum from carrying me through my grief because I didn't trust it…didn't control it. The great posthumous lesson of Mikey and John went unlearned for a half-dozen years. It would take something bigger and older to penetrate my teflon ego. Something as big as a mountain range, as old as a desert.

Something like the Tour Divide.

Like a younger Grace Ragland, the mountains in the north thrash against gravity. The Rockies are majestic and proud, thrusting their defiant granite shields against a sky that carries the weapons of their destruction. They are big enough to make their own weather, but even they do not own their destinies. They are at the mercy of patient yet merciless wind and water and sun. Mountains do not know they are not in control.

The desert has no such expectations. It has been beaten, dried, and baked for eons. It accepts the sparse gifts it is given and persists without possessing. The desert does not speak, its silence communicates the funereal wisdom that drapes its heart. The desert has let go.

The great mountains that separated the country's water between east and west and formed the basis of this race completely disappeared as I made my thirty-second and final crossing of the Continental Divide. The "divide" wandered aimlessly through the flat desert and crossed my path—a shapeless and pathetic formality—about fifty miles north of the border. It was an inglorious end to the writhing, soaring, omnipresent landmark that inspired so much respect and preparation, but it seemed poetic. No matter the mountain, real or imagined, in the end, all is ground to dust.

The same forces that battle the mountains and sustain the desert did a number on me. Physically, I was blasted by water, wind, sun, gravity, friction, and exhaustion. My soul was even more affected. Mile by mile, this race demolished my arrogance, my pride, my lust for control and validation down to rubble. Meanwhile, it filled my reservoir of gratitude, humility, and love. I may have begun a race, but I would be finishing a journey.

The pain and fatigue that had been mounting over the last forty-one days became non-existent. The energy I had received from dozens of trail angels poured out of me, and I floated along the road like an eagle surfing an updraft, putting my feet on the ground only twice over the final 124 miles. The elements I fought along the way—heat, gravity, wind—tipped their cap and allowed me to pass unmolested. Coyotes and serpents took me for their sister. A voice whispered in my ear, "Let go, let go, let go."

I let go and vanished.

In this Eden where the days lost their names, I became the desert.

As heat radiated in transparent, rising waves above the road, I pulled in amongst the complex of low-slung Border Patrol buildings. The year that I had invested was at its end. The dividends of all the dreaming, the preparing, the training, and the suffering I had poured into the Tour Divide paid out in a lonely outpost on a dusty frontier.

Antelope Wells at last.

There was no finish line, no cheering throngs, no podium. The unenthused government employees present could not have cared less that I **had ridden** a bike from Canada. The only sounds were from beat-up cars that periodically crossed the border and the electric hum of air conditioning. I was elated nonetheless. The elephant that I had been nibbling on for nearly seven weeks was now gone.

Unconsciously, I looked for some method of marking the end, some tangible symbol that I had truly finished. At the end of the Appalachian Trail in Maine, a weather-beaten sign stands atop Mount Katahdin marking the finish of a 2,100-mile trail that starts in Georgia. Hikers who reach the monument after months in the wilderness often break down in tears at the sight of the sign.

A U.S. Customs and Border Protection sign for the Antelope Wells station serves in this capacity for TD racers, but for some reason (probably exhaustion) I ignored it and invented my own completion shrine. A Coke machine beckoned from the shade of one of the buildings. I cast my venerations upon the iconic script of the red and white logo and approached it reverently, as if I had just discovered the Holy Grail. I pulled out my last dollar bill as an offertory, and fed it into a soda machine, imagining the blissful taste of a Coke in my parched mouth as I made my selection. Surely this would be the best Coke I had ever tasted, the distillation of a dream come true.

The Holy Grail ate my dollar and gave nothing in return. I was left with no money and nothing to drink but the hot water in my bottle. I chuckled at the cosmic smackdown. Whoever is in charge of the universe doesn't allow the prideful to stay on the mountaintop for long, reminding us that Mr. Murphy and his law can still reach us at any stage of accomplishment. I leaned against the machine and slid down to sit on the sidewalk, feeling the coolness oozing from the opening where the soda should have come out. I took a swig of hot water and looked up. Two crows were sitting on a telephone wire. I called up to them.

"John. Mike. I did it."

I swear those crows smiled at me.

EPILOGUE

There are those who come away from an adventure like the Tour Divide with a deflation of spirit that looks something like postpartum depression. It is such a large undertaking leading up to the race. Planning, acquiring gear, and training were both mentally and physically stimulating. Doing the race felt like, well, being alive. I suppose the TD attracts that rare personality type which only thrives under extreme duress.

It is no wonder then, that the peculiar personality which does so well in harsh environments tends to fare poorly in the humdrum of everyday life. I guess I fit into this category. When I got back to Alabama, everything seemed bland and lifeless. There was nothing to get up for, so I sunk into a depression. I figured the only way for me to ever maintain emotional balance was to ride as much as possible. After allowing my body to heal for a couple of months, I started to get back into the swing, entering races throughout the fall.

But something wasn't right. My fitness, which had been honed to a razor's edge over the course of the Tour, seemingly disappeared overnight. Even short day trips were exhausting. Although I had never dropped out of a race before, I had to quit a multi-day race in Tennessee. It was just too hard.

The golf ball under my jawbone hadn't gotten smaller, either. I thought it was surely the result of the extreme pounding I was giving my body during the Tour Divide and expected it to fade as I recovered. It did not. A tickling cough and runny nose joined the party and did not go away. Finally, I went to the doctor.

The doctor suggested a biopsy of the lymph node. The biopsy came back benign but the doctor wasn't satisfied. He still wanted to take it out completely. I told him about the Tour Divide and said I didn't think I was yet emotionally strong enough to go under the knife, but promised to reschedule within six weeks.

My body didn't feel like waiting that long. I was awakened one night in November with a raging fever. I took my temperature, which registered 104 degrees. I took some ibuprofen and went back to bed. The next morning, the fever was gone. The pattern repeated for two more nights. On the fourth day, the fever didn't subside.

I called my doctor and he advised me to head straight to the emergency room. The ER doc was unimpressed by my fever and golf ball and was prepared to send me on my way with a prescription for antibiotics. I put my foot down.

"No sir, this is not an infection. Something is wrong. I want to see someone else."

An oncologist took one look at me and admitted me to the hospital immediately. For two weeks, I was confined to a hospital bed while the fever burned and I got weaker and weaker. The fearsome strength I had built over the course of the Tour Divide vaporized as if it was a single matchstick that had been struck. On December 14, 2018, an oncologist finally came to me with the news that I had dreaded, yet expected.

"Grace, you have cancer. Non-Hodgkin's Lymphoma."

Cancer. The dreaded word. The harbinger of death—and not that symbolic bullshit I had pondered out in the desert, either. This was real, final, *put-you-in-the-ground-and-cover-you-with-dirt* kind of death. It would be nice if I could say that my meditations on the subject had prepared me to accept the possible outcome, but that would be a lie. I was scared. The blood in my heart went cold.

"What stage?" I asked.

"It's stage four."

"Stage FOUR?" I whispered. I couldn't speak any louder because I had just been punched in the gut by his words.

"Grace," he said in his authoritative doctor voice, "I know what you're thinking. Stop writing your eulogy for a second and listen to me. This kind of cancer is treatable. There is a very strong likelihood of getting you cancer-free. Given your fitness pre-cancer, there is a good chance of remission. But here's the fine print. It's going to suck. Your hair is going to fall out. You will be miserable, nauseated, and tired all the time. You're going to have to stay home and stay off the bike for a few months while we knock this out of you."

I stared at him in disbelief. This was really happening. Cancer.

The doctor broke my trance. "Grace, we need to get started quickly. Do you understand?"

I nodded hypnotically.

"O.K. then. If you're ready, we'll start today."

I wasn't ready, but we started anyway. Lymph node biopsies. Bone marrow biopsies. Lymphadenectomy. Chemo. The doctors turned me inside out to discover the extent of the cancer. Once they were satisfied that they knew what they were dealing with, they turned the big guns on me. The guns had long, intimidating names like rituximab, cyclophosphamide, hydroxydaunomycin, and vincristine.

Christmas came and went while I was in the hospital. On December 27, I was discharged home to fight on familiar turf. For the next three months, the peripatetic lifestyle that I had built and enjoyed so much came to a halt. If I had been healthy, that in itself would've been a tortuous prison sentence, but in my feeble state, it was welcome, even cozy.

My hair fell out in great clumps. I wore knit beanies to ward off the winter's cold. I became a bird watcher and spent the gray days of January and February studying the various species that frequented my feeders. Two dissolute squirrels raided my feeders with impunity, so I began to shoot at them with a pink BB rifle, making sure not to hit them. The constraints of my self-imposed rules of engagement were soon figured out by the squirrels. Without fear of actual bodily harm, they became mocking in their bravery. I abandoned my war and named them instead, greeting Chuck and Pat each day as they made their rounds.

Chemo was a gauntlet that I had to run every three weeks for six rounds. My regimen was called R-CHOP, which was an anagram of the five drugs used to destroy the cancer. CHOP was an appropriate name. I felt as if I were being chopped alive every twenty-one days.

Still, I persisted through the winter and into March, battling and getting a little stronger with each round. My last round of chemo came on April 1st as the dogwoods and cherry trees were blooming. In a show of defiance, I rode my bike five miles to the cancer center. As I was talking to the oncologist, I told him about the golf ball that started it all, and how it had been a grape when I left Banff. The doctor smiled at me when I asked him if I had cancer all that time.

"Yes," he said, "you did that entire race with cancer."

I can. I will. I am.

Less than two months after my final chemo and a year after I rode out of Banff, Canada on a bicycle, I returned to the Rockies. Colorado is my spirit's home and I wanted to finish my season of cancer there among the mountains. Kirsten at Brush Mountain Lodge hosted me once again just like she did a year earlier when I was a hard-charging racer.

During the Tour Divide, the mountains were definitely playing for the other team, now they were my soul's companions, and I rode without purpose or direction, content to be guided by the moment. I loafed my way up snowy Marshall Pass and pedaled softly among the alpine wildflowers, drinking in the silence and solitude like a tonic. I fished in a cold mountain stream and pulled out a humongous rainbow trout. My hair grew back in sheets of wispy soft white gold, like baby hair. I ate without fear of retching and slept without burden. I had become a child again.

The Tour Divide was a kind of death. I was released from a life dominated by ego and wasteful grasping pride. Over the course of 2,700 miles, it showed me how small I was, how insignificant my attachments. My sense of combating, defeating, and establishing dominion over my world was extinguished. The Tour Divide taught me how to let go.

Cancer, on the other hand, had been a rebirth. It razed what remained of my teetering edifice and gave me a clean slate. It was a renewal of my recognition of the wonder of life and simple virtues like gratitude, and the love of family and friends. Cancer didn't teach me to hold onto things, but to *be*-hold them. Behold the beauty of birds at a backyard feeder. Behold the lush spring wildflowers showing off for the strengthening sun. Behold the desert, the mountains, and all the wonderful people who live along the Tour Divide, displaying generosity and kindness as gorgeous as any wildflower or bird's showy plumage. Behold fleeting gift of life, marvel at its fragility and tenacity, and rejoice.

In the alpenglow of a Rocky Mountain evening, I straddled the bike. Kirsten saw me from the kitchen and came outside.

"Hey lady, where ya goin'?"

I didn't answer, I just pointed toward the horizon and started pedaling.

THE END

www.ingramcontent.com/pod-product-compliance
Lightning Source LLC
LaVergne TN
LVHW041632060526
838200LV00040B/1548